Current
CONTROVERSIES

Developing Nations

Other Books in the Current Controversies Series

Developing Nations

Debra A. Miller, Book Editor

WILLOW INTERNATIONAL LIBRARY

GREENHAVEN PRESS
A part of Gale, Cengage Learning

GALE
CENGAGE Learning·

Detroit • New York • San Francisco • New Haven, Conn • Waterville, Maine • London

Elizabeth Des Chenes, *Managing Editor*

© 2012 Greenhaven Press, a part of Gale, Cengage Learning

Gale and Greenhaven Press are registered trademarks used herein under license.

For more information, contact:
Greenhaven Press
27500 Drake Rd.
Farmington Hills, MI 48331-3535
Or you can visit our Internet site at gale.cengage.com

For product information and technology assistance, contact us at

Gale Customer Support, 1-800-877-4253
For permission to use material from this text or product, submit all requests online at www.cengage.com/permissions

Further permissions questions can be emailed to permissionrequest@cengage.com

Articles in Greenhaven Press anthologies are often edited for length to meet page requirements. In addition, original titles of these works are changed to clearly present the main thesis and to explicitly indicate the author's opinion. Every effort is made to ensure that Greenhaven Press accurately reflects the original intent of the authors. Every effort has been made to trace the owners of copyrighted material.

Cover image © Pete McBridge/National Geographic Society/Corbis.

LIBRARY OF CONGRESS CATALOGING-IN-PUBLICATION DATA

Developing nations / Debra A. Miller, book editor.
   p. cm. -- (Current controversies)
   Summary: "What are the Problems Facing Developing Nations?; Did the Global Financial Crisis Hurt Developing Nations?; Can Democracy Succeed in Developing Nations?; What Can Be Done to Aid the Developing World?"--Provided by publisher.
   Includes bibliographical references and index.
   ISBN 978-0-7377-5614-2 (hardback) -- ISBN 978-0-7377-5615-9 (paperback)
   1. Developing countries--Economic conditions. 2. Global Financial Crisis, 2008-2009. 3. Democracy--Developing countries. I. Miller, Debra A.
   HC59.7.D372 2012
   330.9172'4--dc23
                      2011033272

Printed in the United States of America
1 2 3 4 5 6 7 15 14 13 12 11

Contents

Chapter 2: Did the Global Financial Crisis Hurt Developing Nations?

No: The Global Financial Crisis Did Not Hurt Developing Nations

In recent years, China has built close diplomatic and economic relations with numerous developing countries using what the Chinese call soft power—basically, by providing training programs and foreign aid. This use of soft power increasingly is a tool used by China to promote the anti-democratic Chinese model of government, and China may ultimately mount a serious challenge to democracy in the developing world.

Chapter 4: What Can Be Done to Aid the Developing World?

Rich nations and international institutions such as the International Monetary Fund and the World Bank have imposed policies of structural adjustment, trade liberalization, and conservative macroeconomic management on many developing nations in recent decades, but these policies have failed to reduce poverty or promote economic growth. Poverty has been reduced mainly in countries like China, which rejected these policies and achieved rapid economic growth, despite the existence of widespread government corruption. Population Control Policies in

Foreword

By definition, controversies are "discussions of questions in which opposing opinions clash" (*Webster's Twentieth Century Dictionary Unabridged*). Few would deny that controversies are a pervasive part of the human condition and exist on virtually every level of human enterprise. Controversies transpire between individuals and among groups, within nations and between nations. Controversies supply the grist necessary for progress by providing challenges and challengers to the status quo. They also create atmospheres where strife and warfare can flourish. A world without controversies would be a peaceful world; but it also would be, by and large, static and prosaic.

The Series' Purpose

The purpose of the Current Controversies series is to explore many of the social, political, and economic controversies dominating the national and international scenes today. Titles selected for inclusion in the series are highly focused and specific. For example, from the larger category of criminal justice, Current Controversies deals with specific topics such as police brutality, gun control, white collar crime, and others. The debates in Current Controversies also are presented in a useful, timeless fashion. Articles and book excerpts included in each title are selected if they contribute valuable, long-range ideas to the overall debate. And wherever possible, current information is enhanced with historical documents and other relevant materials. Thus, while individual titles are current in focus, every effort is made to ensure that they will not become quickly outdated. Books in the Current Controversies series will remain important resources for librarians, teachers, and students for many years.

In addition to keeping the titles focused and specific, great care is taken in the editorial format of each book in the series. Book introductions and chapter prefaces are offered to provide background material for readers. Chapters are organized around several key questions that are answered with diverse opinions representing all points on the political spectrum. Materials in each chapter include opinions in which authors clearly disagree as well as alternative opinions in which authors may agree on a broader issue but disagree on the possible solutions. In this way, the content of each volume in Current Controversies mirrors the mosaic of opinions encountered in society. Readers will quickly realize that there are many viable answers to these complex issues. By questioning each author's conclusions, students and casual readers can begin to develop the critical thinking skills so important to evaluating opinionated material.

Current Controversies is also ideal for controlled research. Each anthology in the series is composed of primary sources taken from a wide gamut of informational categories including periodicals, newspapers, books, US and foreign government documents, and the publications of private and public organizations. Readers will find factual support for reports, debates, and research papers covering all areas of important issues. In addition, an annotated table of contents, an index, a book and periodical bibliography, and a list of organizations to contact are included in each book to expedite further research.

Perhaps more than ever before in history, people are confronted with diverse and contradictory information. During the Persian Gulf War, for example, the public was not only treated to minute-to-minute coverage of the war, it was also inundated with critiques of the coverage and countless analyses of the factors motivating US involvement. Being able to sort through the plethora of opinions accompanying today's major issues, and to draw one's own conclusions, can be a complicated and frustrating struggle. It is the editors' hope that Current Controversies will help readers with this struggle.

Introduction

"Despite the long litany of troubles still facing poor countries, experts . . . agree that the developing world has made significant progress during the last half century."

Much is written about the many problems faced by developing countries. High rates of poverty, hunger, and malnutrition still plague many poor nations, as well as a host of other challenges involving critical matters such as health, education, economic development, and the environment. Yet despite the long litany of troubles still facing poor countries, experts also agree that the developing world has made significant progress during the last half century.

Development Progress

According to the United States Agency for International Development (USAID), an independent federal agency that provides governmental foreign aid and development assistance to struggling parts of the world, developing countries have made meaningful strides in important areas such as income, health, life expectancy, literacy, and political freedom. On average, the agency reports, people in the developing world are healthier and live longer than they did several decades ago. One of the clearest measures of health is life expectancy rates, and by this measure, most developing countries have made vast improvements. In the 1950s, some 27 percent of the world's population lived in countries where life expectancy averaged less than forty years, but by 2000, only 4 percent lived in countries where it was less than fifty years—a 60 percent decrease since mid-century. Women have increased their life expectancy more than men, and they now live about 4.2 years longer than men on average. This improvement in life expectancy has been based largely on a decline in infant mortality. Between 1970 and 1999, the number of babies who died within a year of their birth declined from 158 per every 1,000 babies born to 63 per 1,000 born. The developing world now has an average infant mortality rate of 69 for every 1,000 live births—approximately the rate industrial countries had in 1950.

In addition, fewer people today go hungry in the developing world than in the 1950s. At the beginning of the twenty-first century, approximately 432 million people (or about 7 percent of the world's population) lived in countries where the average daily intake was less than twenty-two hundred calories—the minimum amount considered necessary to maintain health. This compares to almost 1.8 billion (or about 57 percent of the world's population) at the mid-century mark.

Developing countries saw gains in education as well. According to USAID, as of 1950, 35 percent of people aged fifteen and older in developing countries were literate, but by 2000, this number had grown to 74 percent. That means 2.4 billion people in the developing world can read, compared with only 366 million in 1950. The dramatic improvements in education are the result of efforts to enroll children in school. The number of enrolled students in developing countries grew rapidly between 1950 and 2000, both at the primary and secondary school levels. Improvements in primary school enrollments came largely from enrolling girls as well as boys, particularly in Arab countries where educating girls was long considered unnecessary. Most remarkable, however, is the increase in secondary level students. In 1950, only the children of the very elite could hope to have access to a secondary level education, but by 1997, 52 percent of children in the relevant age group were enrolled in secondary schools. This puts developing countries about forty years behind industrial countries, which had a 50 percent secondary enrollment rate in 1955.

The developing world also has seen improvements in other measures of well-being. One measure of poverty used by the World Bank, for example, is $1 a day per person. Using this measure, some studies have documented a rapid decline in the percentage of the world population living in poverty—from 55 percent in 1950 to 20 percent in 1998. Another area important to well-being is political freedom. As of 1950, much of the developing world was ruled by autocratic leaders like Soviet leader Joseph Stalin and Communist China leader Mao Zedong. Since then, however, many developing nations have embraced representative democracy as a way to live more freely without overbearing government control.

Uneven Success

Of course, some developing nations have fared better than others. Asia is an obvious bright spot—a region led by amazing economic growth and development in China, today one of the world's strongest and fastest growing economies. One of the most dramatic examples of progress, however, is South Korea, which in the 1950s was a very poor, rural nation whose economy was dependent on agriculture yet was struggling to feed its population. Since then, the nation has transformed itself into an urban, industrialized nation with rapid and sustained economic growth. It is often called an Asian Tiger because of this economic success.

However, millions of people in other developing regions still suffer from hunger, poverty, disease, and other afflictions that marked Third World nations in the past. For example, although the world produces abundant quantities of food—enough to feed the entire world—the problem of hunger and malnutrition has not been eradicated. During the years 1997–1999, thirty-six countries still had a per-person intake of less than twenty-two hundred calories a day. As of 2010, the Food and Agriculture Organization of the United Nations estimated that a total of 925 million people in developing countries were undernourished and experiencing food insecurity—a shortage of food because they lack the income or resources to buy or produce enough food to feed themselves. Many of the poorest, hungriest, and least developed countries are in Sub-Saharan Africa, North Africa, Central Asia, and the Middle East, but some, such as Haiti, can be found in other parts of the world.

The viewpoints in *Current Controversies: Developing Nations* discuss the status of developing countries in today's world. Viewpoint authors identify many of the challenges still facing developing nations, as well as the effects of the global recession, whether democracy can succeed in these areas, and what can be done to aid the developing world in the future.

CHAPTER 1

What Are the Problems Facing Developing Nations?

Chapter Preface

The United States provides billions of dollars in aid to a variety of foreign countries, many of them developing nations. A large portion of this aid comes from the federal government, either in the form of military or economic assistance. US military assistance is controlled by the US Department of Defense, while government economic aid is channeled largely through a special aid agency, the United States Agency for International Development (USAID), but also through the US State Department, the US Department of Agriculture, and other federal agencies. The US foreign aid program has been criticized by some as less than generous, but private organizations and individuals from the United States also distribute significant sums in aid throughout the world.

US foreign aid is a relatively recent phenomenon. Early in US history, the government simply did not distribute any type of aid to other countries. The first program of foreign aid occurred during World War I (1914–1918) when the US government contributed $387 million to help the war-torn country of Belgium. At war's end, an American Relief Administration continued to provide food and health aid to various European countries to help them recover from the devastation of the war. A similar pattern emerged in World War II (1939–1945), when aid was first provided to Great Britain and other European nations through President Franklin D. Roosevelt's Lend-Lease program, and then continued after the war with the Marshall Plan—a large-scale economic program designed to help rebuild the countries of Europe. Over 3.5 years, the US government distributed about $12.5 billion through the Marshall Plan, mostly to Great Britain, France, and West Germany. Various temporary agencies continued the now-established tradition of providing foreign aid over the next couple of decades, until 1961, when President John F. Kennedy helped to create the USAID to oversee US foreign assistance programs. Since then, US foreign aid contributions have increased each year with the stated purpose of promoting economic growth, environmental sustainability, poverty alleviation, and democratic and economic freedom. In fiscal year 2007, the latest year for which statistics are available, the US government spent $13 billion for military assistance and $26.9 billion for economic aid.

Controversy surrounds the US foreign aid program, however. Critics complain that although America gives more in foreign aid than any other country, it gives the least of the twenty-two most-developed nations when foreign aid is calculated as a percentage of the US gross domestic product (GDP), a measure of the country's total economic output or wealth. Compared with Denmark, often called the world's most generous nation because it allocates 1.01 percent of its GDP to foreign aid, the United States gives away only 0.1 percent of US GDP. In addition, critics say that the United States often provides more aid to nations that are strategically or militarily important to US foreign and defense policy, instead of prioritizing the countries that are most in need of development aid. In recent years, for example, about one-third of all US aid, both military and economic, went to Israel and Egypt, neither of which is a developing country. In both countries, the majority of the US aid was used to provide military arms. Two other countries deemed to be important to the United States for strategic reasons—Iraq and Afghanistan—also received huge amounts of US assistance, both military and economic.

One way the US government responds to these criticisms is to point out the large amount of aid provided by private sources in the country. USAID, for example, argues that private aid should be included in the estimates of how much the United States donates in foreign economic aid. In 2007, the amount of private money given away to foreign countries, according to some sources, totaled more than $24 billion, almost as much as the United States donated in official government economic aid. This private money comes from various sources; estimates for 2007 include foundations ($3.4 billion), private charities ($9.7 billion), churches and religious organizations ($4.5 billion), universities ($1.7 billion), and corporations ($4.9 billion).

In addition, many US aid experts say remittances—money sent by foreign workers in the United States to their home countries—should be counted as foreign aid because they greatly benefit developing economies. Although difficult to calculate with great accuracy, the amount sent in remittances by immigrant workers in the United States to other countries is estimated to be quite large. According to the Center for Global Prosperity, for example, US remittances to developing countries in 2008 totaled $96.8 billion. Mexico received the largest share of US remittances—approximately $24.2 billion in 2008—followed by India ($10.6 billion) and the Phillipines ($10.4 billion). In fact, the United States is the largest source of remittances to the developing world; US remittances account for more than half of the total remittances sent to developing countries.

Despite the flow of foreign aid into the developing world, however, many developing countries continue to struggle with a host of serious challenges. The authors of the viewpoints in this chapter describe some of the problems facing developing nations.

Hunger in Developing Nations Is Still a Serious Problem

ActionAid

ActionAid is an international South Africa-based agency whose aim is to fight poverty worldwide.

This September [2010], leaders are gathering in New York to assess progress on the UN's [United Nations] Millennium Development Goals [MDGs] for halving extreme poverty and hunger by 2015. On hunger, the MDGs commit leaders to reducing by half the proportion of people who are undernourished and the proportion of children who are underweight. These targets are, quite literally, a matter of life and death for the one billion people who struggle on a daily basis to avoid starvation.

Going Backwards: The Billion Hungry

With only five years to go, how is the world doing? The bitter truth is that the world is going backwards on hunger. If massive gains in China are excluded from the picture, then global hunger has risen back to exactly the same level in 2009 as it was in 1990. This means that 500 million more people are chronically malnourished than if the UN goal had been achieved.

The two regions which are home to the largest numbers of hungry people, South Asia and Sub-Saharan Africa, have lost the most ground in the wake of the food and financial crises. In South Asia, the prevalence of hunger surpassed the MDG 1990 baseline levels last year [2009], gripping more than one in five of the region's people. Nearly half of South Asian children remain malnourished, a situation little changed from 1990—indefensible considering the region's per capita income has tripled in the same period.

In Sub-Saharan Africa, alarmingly, just under a third of the total population was chronically hungry by 2009—up by two percentage points, from 30 percent in 2006. Worst of all, food security is predicted to deteriorate further in Africa, to the point that nearly 50 percent of Africans could be going without enough food by 2020.

The bitter truth is that the world is going backwards on hunger.

However, the news is not all bad. Governments are beginning to re-invest in agriculture, albeit from a very low base. Seven countries improved their score on budgetary allocations to agriculture between last year and this year. The food and financial crises have also spurred some improvements to social assistance programmes, which often make the difference between vulnerability and destitution when times get tough. Although such programmes are still tiny in most developing countries, twelve countries (Burundi, Ethiopia, The Gambia, Ghana, Kenya, Senegal, Sierra Leone, Uganda, China, Nepal, Pakistan, Guatemala and Haiti) improved their score this year for social safety net coverage, while only a handful went down.

Counting the Cost

Even before the food and financial crises pushed hunger to unprecedented highs, malnutrition was the underlying cause of nearly 4.5 million child deaths every year. An extra 1.2 million children could die unnecessarily between now and 2015, partly as a result of setbacks on hunger.

Large as it is, the loss of life caused by hunger is dwarfed by the invisible and permanent loss of human potential. Childhood hunger causes irreversible damage to mental and physical capacity, cutting a person's lifetime earnings by as much as 20 percent and reducing overall economic output. ActionAid estimates that failure to meet the MDG of halving hunger is costing developing countries over $450 billion per year in lost GDP [gross national product, the measure of a country's total economic output]—more than 10 times the amount the UN estimates would be needed to achieve the MDG hunger targets.

The two regions ... [with] the largest numbers of hungry people, South Asia and Sub-Saharan Africa, have lost the most ground in the wake of the food and financial crises.

The Great Hunger Divide

The country-by-country analysis on MDG1 hunger targets presented in the HungerFREE scorecard shows a great divide between countries that are more or less on track and those that are very far from it.

Of the 28 developing countries measured, only 8 are on track to meet both the hunger targets, 20 countries are off track to meet one or both of the MDG targets. Of these, 12 are actually moving backwards not forward on one or both of the MDG targets: i.e. an increasing proportion of the population is hungry. The Democratic Republic of Congo is the worst performer, with a staggering 76 percent of their population hungry, representing a fourfold increase since 1990—the worst hunger record in the world. Pakistan, another country backsliding, has seen the proportion of hungry rise from one in four to an estimated one in two during the same period.

And it isn't just the poorest, the war-torn and disaster-struck countries of the world that are not doing well. Some of the world's 'wealthier' countries are shockingly off track. In India, one of the world's emerging recent global economic 'successes', 1 in 5 of the population are hungry, and close to 50 percent of all children are malnourished.

20 countries have been moving forward far too slowly to meet the 2015 deadline; for instance, according to ActionAid's projections, Kenya and Senegal won't meet the hunger reduction target until 2124 and 2060, respectively.

On the other side of the divide, 13 of the 28 HungerFREE countries in this study have shown what is possible and are on track to meet one or both of the goals—demonstrating that the goals are more than achievable.

Brazil, China, Ghana, Malawi and Vietnam are among those that have slashed hunger rates—and are the top five performers on the HungerFREE scorecard. Brazil has more than halved the prevalence of underweight children in less than 10 years. China has also made impressive progress and met their MDG1 obligations well ahead of time. Ghana cut hunger levels by 75 percent between 1990 and 2004. In Vietnam, the rate of underweight children has plummeted from close to 45 percent in the early 1990s to fewer than 20 percent today. Similarly Malawi has also put a decisive end to years of recurring famine, reducing the number of people requiring food aid from over 4.5 million in 2004 to less than 150,000 in 2009.

Of the 28 developing countries measured, only 8 are on track to meet both the hunger targets, 20 countries are off track to meet one or both of the MDG targets.

What Needs to Happen?

How have some governments, including some in very poor countries of the world, managed to tackle hunger and poverty so effectively, whereas others have failed? And why are some governments and the world not doing more? . . .

The 2010 HungerFREE scorecard shows that there are some simple steps that would make it both possible and affordable to halve hunger by 2015.

The scorecard assesses developing countries on four areas of public action: legal commitment to food as a right, investment in agriculture and social protection, and gender equality.

What is striking in this analysis is the overlap between those countries which have made huge progress on hunger and the high scorers on their policy actions. On the flipside, there is a conspicuous correlation between countries that are low deliverers on policy actions and have high hunger numbers.

By investing more in local agriculture, governments can feed their people and also regenerate rural economies. Recent research has pointed to the vital role that agriculture played in China's initial take-off. Agriculture was estimated to have contributed to poverty reduction four times more than growth in manufacturing or service sectors. As China's story demonstrates, the biggest impact on reducing hunger and poverty is achieved when governments focus on supporting the small-scale farmers who grow the majority of staple foods consumed locally. There are particularly massive gains to be reaped from investing in women farmers, who currently receive hardly any credit or extension advice and seldom enjoy secure rights over land.

The HungerFREE scorecard also shows that well-designed social assistance programmes, such as public works employment, cash transfers, food rations, and free school meals, are an important hunger-fighting weapon.

Recent country-level evidence analysed by ActionAid shows significant increases in the most serious form of child hunger (wasting, or short-term weight loss) since the food crisis struck in 2007/8. This demonstrates exactly how vulnerable children are to reduced food intake in times of distress, and therefore how important it is to put basic safety nets in place.

Safety nets are also important to help small farmers keep planting and harvesting through tough times, avoiding the distress sales of livestock and land that so often push vulnerable families over the brink into chronic hunger and destitution.

Brazil, our overall chart topper for the second time in a row, has expanded welfare coverage dramatically in recent years. Increases in the minimum wage and a national cash transfer programme have been introduced alongside subsidised credit and procurement programmes that support smallholder farmers. Taken together, these measures are widely recognised as having a phenomenal impact on reducing Brazil's once infamous inequalities—with child hunger rates slashed by over 50 per cent in little over 10 years.

Legal commitment to food as a basic human right can help to create political pressure on governments to make hunger a priority. Alongside this, strong rural institutions that give the poorest some influence over government actions are indispensable.

Rich countries also have a critical part to play. They need to change policies that aggravate hunger in the developing world, such as targets and subsidies that promote the use of biofuels made from food crops. European targets for biofuels expansion could push prices of grains and food oils 15 percent higher by 2017, according to the OECD [Organisation for Economic Co-operation and Development].

The UN's Intergovernmental Panel on Climate Change (IPCC) predicts that global warming could put 50 million extra people at risk of hunger by 2020, rising to an additional 266 million by 2080. Rich countries need to cut their greenhouse gas emissions, and provide the minimum US $200 billion needed annually to enable poor countries to fight climate change.

Finally, rich countries need to live up to their many promises to increase financing for agriculture in the developing world. Almost all donors are starting from a very low base of severe underinvestment in agriculture. But the HungerFREE

Scorecard gives credit to those countries that have pledged money to agriculture since the food crisis. The 2009 G8 [nations with the top eight economies] pledge of US$22 billion, over 3 years, to support developing country farmers and fight hunger is a critical step forward, as is the recognition that the key to solving the food crisis lies in investing in smallholder farmers. However, according to ActionAid's calculation, only around US$6 billion of this is new money rather than recycled pledges—and it is still not clear how or when the money will be spent.

Toward a Hunger-Free World

As global populations grow, the fight is on over how to solve the global crisis in resources. The massive overconsumption of energy and other environmental resources in the North [i.e., the Northern Hemisphere], combined with the looming impacts of climate change and decades of neglect of impoverished small farmers in the developing world, could lead to an explosion of food shortages and hunger in decades to come. We need bold plans to build vibrant and sustainable farming economies in poor countries: so that hunger becomes yesterday's news, not tomorrow's headline.

To meet the MDG1 goal of halving hunger, world leaders . . . must:

1. *Invest in farmers*

   • Agree [on] national plans that are sufficiently bold and ambitious to halve hunger by 2015, backed by costed, time-bound actions and firm financing commitments by both governments and donors.

   • The UN estimates that at least US$40 billion in additional funding will be required annually to halve hunger by 2015; donors should set out a timetable and mechanism to meet their part of the need and guarantee that no country with a good plan for achieving the hunger goal is thwarted for lack of resources.

- National plans should focus on supporting poor farmers, particularly women, in order to maximize poverty and hunger reduction impacts.

- National plans should expand social protection programmes to ensure that households don't fall into hunger when prices rise or harvests fail.

2. *Act on climate change*

- Commit to a reduction of at least 40 percent of developed country emissions by 2020 in order to keep temperatures below the danger zone of a 1.5 degrees Celsius increase in temperatures.

- Increase their climate financing pledges to cover the minimum US$200 billion needed annually in developing countries, ensure their funding is new money (that is, doesn't reduce other aid), and specify a source.

3. *Change course on biofuels*

- The European Union and United States must eliminate targets and subsidies for biofuel production, which directly undermine food security and have little or no environmental benefit.

Death from Preventable Infectious Diseases in Developing Nations Is a Continuing Problem

Global Health Council

The Global Health Council is a membership alliance dedicated to saving lives by improving health throughout the world.

Diseases caused by bacteria, viruses, fungi and other parasites are major causes of death, disability, and social and economic disruption for millions of people. Despite the existence of safe and effective interventions, many people lack access to needed preventive and treatment care. The lost productivity, missed educational opportunities and high health-care costs caused by infectious diseases directly impact families and communities.

Infections are prevalent in developing countries, where co-infection is common. The adverse impact of infectious diseases is most severe among the poorest people, who have the fewest material, physical and financial resources to draw from and limited or no access to integrated health care, prevention tools and medications.

Infectious diseases raise awareness of our global vulnerability, the need for strong health care systems and the potentially broad and borderless impact on disease.

- Over 9.5 million people die each year due to infectious diseases—nearly all live in developing countries.

- Children are particularly vulnerable to infectious diseases. Pneumonia, diarrhea and malaria are leading causes of death among children under age 5; cerebral malaria can cause permanent mental impairment.

- Infectious diseases are also destructive to the health of adults, causing disability, a diminished quality of life, decreased productivity or death.

- *Co-infection.* People infected with one infectious disease become more susceptible to other diseases. Examples include: HIV/AIDS co-infection with tuberculosis or malaria co-infection with multiple neglected diseases.

- *Interventions.* Illness and death from infectious diseases are particularly tragic because they are largely preventable and treatable with available interventions.

Progress on infectious diseases includes:

- Efforts to achieve the sixth Millennium Development Goal (MDG), which focuses on stopping and reversing the spread of infectious diseases by 2015.

- Regional progress against infectious diseases, such as:

- A 91 percent reduction in deaths resulting from measles in Africa between 2000 and 2006.

- The Eastern Mediterranean region, which includes Afghanistan, Pakistan, Somalia, and the Sudan, has seen a 90 percent reduction in measles deaths from 2000 and 2007.

- The attainment of successful treatment of tuberculosis among 85 percent of patients in the Western Pacific and Southeast Asia during 2005.

- The near eradication of polio and guinea worm disease, and lower prevalence of several other tropical diseases over the past few decades.

- A renewed interest in the research and development of new diagnostics, vaccines and drug treatments.

- *Increased funding* could help eradicate, eliminate and control diseases, preventing millions of deaths and improving the lives of many millions more.

Environmental Damage Caused by Rich Nations Is Harming Developing Nations

Bob Sanders

Bob Sanders is a University of California–Berkeley science writer.

The environmental damage caused by rich nations disproportionately impacts poor nations and costs them more than their combined foreign debt, according to a first-ever global accounting of the dollar costs of countries' ecological footprints.

The study, led by former University of California [UC], Berkeley, research fellow Thara Srinivasan, assessed the impacts of agricultural intensification and expansion, deforestation, overfishing, loss of mangrove swamps and forests, ozone depletion and climate change during a 40-year period, from 1961 to 2000. In the case of climate change and ozone depletion, the researchers also estimated the impacts that may be felt through the end of this century.

A Debt to Poor Nations

"At least to some extent, the rich nations have developed at the expense of the poor and, in effect, there is a debt to the poor," said coauthor Richard B. Norgaard, an ecological economist and UC Berkeley professor of energy and resources. "That, perhaps, is one reason that they are poor. You don't see it until you do the kind of accounting that we do here."

The calculation of the ecological footprints of the world's low-, middle- and high-income nations drew upon more than a decade of assessments by environmental economists who have tried to attach monetary figures to environmental damage, plus data from the recent United Nations Millennium Ecosystem Assessment and World Bank reports.

Because of the monumental nature of such an accounting, the UC Berkeley researchers limited their study to six areas of human activity. Impacts of activities that are difficult to assess, such as loss of habitat and biodiversity and the effects of industrial pollution, were ignored. Because of this, the researchers said that the estimated financial costs in the report are a minimum.

Rich nations have developed at the expense of the poor and, in effect, there is a debt to the poor.

"We think the measured impact is conservative. And given that it's conservative, the numbers are very striking," said Srinivasan, who is now at the Pacific Ecoinformatics and Computational Ecology (PEACE) Lab in Berkeley. "To our knowledge, our study is the first to really examine where nations' ecological footprints are falling, and it is an interesting contrast to the wealth of nations."

Srinivasan, Norgaard and their colleagues reported their results this week [mid-January 2008] in the early online edition of the journal *Proceedings of the National Academy of Sciences.*

"In the past half century, humanity has transformed our natural environment at an unprecedented speed and scale," Srinivasan said, noting that the Earth's population doubled in the past 50 years to 6.5 billion as the average per-capita gross world product also doubled. "What we don't know is which nations around the world are really driving the ecological damages and which are paying the price."

Environmental Costs

Norgaard said that the largest environmental impact by far is from climate change, which has been assessed in previous studies. The current study broadens the assessment to include other significant human activities with environmental costs and thus provides a context for the earlier studies.

The study makes clear, for example, that while deforestation and agricultural intensification primarily impact the host country, the impacts from climate change and ozone depletion are spread widely over all nations.

"Low-income countries will bear significant burdens from climate change and ozone depletion. But these environmental problems have been overwhelmingly driven by emission of greenhouse gases and ozone-depleting chemicals by the rest of the world," Srinivasan said.

Climate change is expected to increase the severity of storms and extreme weather, including prolonged droughts and flooding, with an increase in infectious diseases. Ozone depletion mostly impacts health, with increases expected in cancer rates, cataracts and blindness. All of these will affect vulnerable low-income countries disproportionately.

Low-income countries will bear significant burdens from climate change and ozone depletion ... overwhelmingly driven by emission of greenhouse gases and ozone-depleting chemicals by the rest of the world.

In addition to climate change and ozone depletion, over-fishing and conversion of mangrove swamps to shrimp farming are areas in which rich nations burden poor countries.

"Seafood derived from depleted fish stocks in low-income country waters ultimately ends up on the plates of consumers in middle-income and rich countries," Srinivasan said. "The situation is similar for farmed shrimp. For such a small, rare habitat, mangroves, when cut down, exact a surprisingly large cost borne primarily by the poor- and middle-income countries."

The primary cost is loss of storm protection, which some say was a major factor in the huge loss of life from 2005's tsunami in Southeast Asia.

When all these [environmental] impacts are added up, the portion ... that is falling on the low-income countries is greater than the financial debt recognized for low-income countries.

Deforestation, on the other hand, can exacerbate flooding and soil erosion, affect the water cycle and offshore fisheries and lead to the loss of recreation and of non-timber products such as latex and food sources. Agricultural intensification can lead to drinking water contamination by pesticides and fertilizers, pollution of streams, salinization of croplands and biodiversity loss, among other impacts.

The Impact on Poor Countries

When all these impacts are added up, the portion of the footprint of high-income nations that is falling on the low-income countries is greater than the financial debt recognized for low-income countries, which has a net present value of 1.8 trillion in 2005 international dollars, Srinivasan said. (International dollars are U.S. dollars adjusted to account for the different purchasing power of different currencies.) "The ecological debt could more than offset the financial debt of low-income nations," she said.

Interestingly, middle-income nations may have an impact on poor nations that is equivalent to the impact of rich nations, the study shows. While poor nations impact other income tiers also, their effect on rich nations is less than a third of the impact that the rich have on the poor.

Norgaard admits that "there will be a lot of controversy about whether you can even do this kind of study and whether we did it right. A lot of that will just be trying to blindside the study, to not think about it. What we really want to do is challenge people to think about it. And if anything, if you don't believe it, do it yourself and do it better."

Private-Sector Corruption Is Growing in Developing Nations

Andrew Bast

Andrew Bast is a journalist who has reported for several publications, including Newsweek, *the* Village Voice, *and the* New York Times.

M exico's Carlos Slim is emblematic of an emerging market tycoon who's contributing to a top-heavy economy.

Worth more than $60 billion, magnate Carlos Slim Helú is the richest man in the world, which makes him a titan in Mexico. His vast network of companies constitutes 42 percent of the country's benchmark stock index. América Móvil, his cellular-phone empire, controls more than 70 percent of the domestic market. And while Mexico has made one of the most remarkable recoveries from the financial crisis—the International Monetary Fund [IMF] just revised its growth forecast up to 4.5 percent this year [2010], a third higher than its superpower neighbor to the north, and exports are booming, up 44 percent in May [2010]—economists argue that Slim's success actually comes at the cost of Mexico's growth.

Nobody's suggesting anything illegal is afoot, but the concentration of business wealth and power among just a few makes economists "talk about Mexico as if it has given up a few percentage points of GDP [gross domestic product, a measure of a country's total economic output] growth," says Raghuram Rajan, a former chief economist of the IMF.

President Felipe Calderón says that monopolies are forcing a 40 percent premium on Mexicans for everyday goods and services. Likewise, credit for consumers and small businesses is abysmally low, stunting enterprise. Meanwhile, Slim's firms, along with those run by a handful of other modern-day tycoons in the country—like retailer and banker Ricardo Salinas's Grupo Salinas or the Azcárraga family's media empire—deliver eye-popping gains. In other words, Slim may be great, but if he's all that Mexico's got, that's no good.

Emerging markets may be the most promising global investments, but many are lopsided and some even corrupt.

Corruption in Emerging Economies

Surveying the landscape of emerging markets today, the "Slim syndrome" is one of the foremost dangers developing economies face. In the same way the technology boom fueled the 1990s, emerging markets (averaging 6 percent growth) have been the relentless drivers of the global economy over the last decade. However, without a sea change in the way these countries do business, the spectacular ride could soon come to a stunted end. Fifteen years ago the backroom privilege of big-time industrialists was known as crony capitalism, and its insidious grip brought down several of the so-called Asian tigers. Today, the situation is different. Interviews with some two dozen economists, bankers, and consultants working in emerging markets paint a portrait that would better be called "crooked capitalism." Emerging markets may be the most promising global investments, but many are lopsided and some even corrupt.

Monopolies, graft [extortion], and massive infusions of state spending are resulting in low competition and unsustainable gains, and the heavier hand of government is carrying these problems into the future. For countries like Mexico, India, China, Russia, Indonesia, and several other developing economies, "this is the fork in the road," says Ruchir Sharma, head of emerging markets at Morgan Stanley [an investment firm]. The export-led growth strategies that fueled the boom were, "in large part facilitated by the fact that the cost of capital was very cheap across the globe." Investors poured money into manufacturing sectors that boomed off the back of cheap labor, and a new class of oligarchs like Slim rose by snapping up state assets on the cheap. But now the cost of capital is rising, wages are going up, and the once hungry consumer stalwarts like the U.S. and Europe are facing anemic growth, likely for years to come. To prepare for the long haul, emerging-market economies need to become more competitive domestically and crack down on corruption. The problem is that, as Sharma argues, instead of an appetite for reform, success has often sparked a turn toward complacency.

Crony capitalism involved an incestuous relationship between industrialists, politicians, and banks. By the late 1990s family-run firms in South Korea, Indonesia, Thailand, and Malaysia had grown into far-flung global enterprises, often fueled by sweetheart loans from well-rewarded friends in government and banks that were part of the family empire, too. The debts rung up under this system were massive, often uncountable and untraceable, and the whole system came crashing down in the Asian financial crisis of 1997–98. Economies and currencies collapsed. The International Monetary Fund intervened with more than $100 billion in bailouts, broke up many of the corrupt banks, and pressed many of the stricken conglomerates to reform their ways. In fact, many firms have. "During the recent global financial crisis, many emerging markets faced something of a stress test of their cronyism," says Simon Johnson, former chief economist of the IMF. Many bounced back quickly because they've improved their macroeconomic policies, and Johnson says "there are better governance structures, but these problems are still very real."

The obvious answer to monopolies is to bust them up or regulate them into submission. Analysts often point out that America was still a developing economy when, in the early 20th century, the government broke up the Gilded Age's commercial empires. But today there is precious little momentum behind monopoly reform. There may be a simpler solution, says Charles Ormiston, head of Asia strategy at Bain & Co. [a business strategy consulting firm]: "Allow more foreign competition," particularly in sectors dominated by the large export firms, creating a more dynamic and fluid market to spur innovation and growth.

Instead of an appetite for reform, [economic] success has often sparked a turn toward complacency.

There are some positive signs. Suvojoy Sengupta, a partner with Booz & Co. [a business management consulting firm], says that often "a good relationship with the government is still an important one," but reforms in India have introduced remarkable competition, especially in the automobile and insurance sectors. He says "it's forced the erstwhile crony capitalists to get their acts together." And obviously, with competition, prices drop, which is good for consumers. Brazil's antitrust regulator is considered by many to be one of the world's most lackluster, but its current head, Arthur Badin, is fighting for legislation to add muscle to the office and is targeting the construction industry, where infrastructure dollars are pouring in and big firms hold significant control.

The real question is, will these economies take up reform before the corrosive effects of monopolies begin to slow them down in the coming decade? After all, the massive investment in infrastructure today is, at least in theory, supposed to build a platform for a thriving and dynamic economy for decades to come. But if that process ends up expanding the power of the monopolists, the Slim syndrome will only become more acute.

Developing Nations Are Most Likely to Experience Civil Wars

David Elborn

The late David Elborn was the creator of the Eliminatewar forever.org weblog campaign, an effort devoted to eliminating war by providing an alternative, more civilized procedure for nations to resolve their differences.

In the past there have been civil wars about ethnic and religious hatred (e.g. Northern Ireland and Serbia).

In the world today the nations most susceptible to civil wars are poor countries with a lack of economic development who rely on primary commodities for export, and who have a low stagnant economy with an unequally distributed per capita income.

There are 58 countries with a combined population of one billon that fit into this category and history tells us that they are very vulnerable to civil war.

Social Conditions and Civil War

The social conditions that, in the main, lead to civil war follow a typical pattern.

Poor governance, coupled with an economy in the doldrums.

High unemployment. Hundreds of thousands of people living in abject poverty and suffering, and dying of malnutrition and diseases such as malaria and HIV/AIDS.

Political leaders living in luxury (usually in palatial homes built by their former colonial masters), surrounded by servants and armed guards.

David Elborn, "How We Can Eliminate Civil Wars," eliminatewarforever.org, 2008–2009. Copyright © 2009 by David Elborn. Reproduced by permission.

A feeling of hopelessness among the majority of the populace prevails.

A charismatic rebel leader rises up against the government protesting against the chronic social conditions.

In response, the government substantially increases military spending (can be as high as 6% of GDP [gross domestic product, the measure of a nation's wealth]). . . . In 2006, 85% of weapon export sales were made by the UK [United Kingdom], US and Russia, of which 70% were supplied to developing countries.

Neighbouring countries become jittery and to counter, increase their military expenditure as well, much to the delight of weapon manufacturers.

> *The social conditions that . . . lead to civil war follow a typical pattern.*

The rebel leader raises money for military equipment through various sources, e.g. the sale of illicit commodities (drugs), extortion rackets and kidnapping of business people for ransom (often in the oil industry), trading in commodities like diamonds and timber, donations from diasporas [those who live outside their homeland], and neighbouring countries hostile to the government of the country concerned. The weapon manufacturers ask no questions and supply arms to the rebel leader.

The top socio-economic group, the well-educated people, flee the country and find refuge and jobs in developed nations.

Civil War Is a Human Catastrophe

The rebel leader recruits an army mainly consisting of bored, unemployed, uneducated young males full of testosterone who are easily manipulated by propaganda. This brings excitement and purpose into their lives and they find having adequate food, clothing and shelter comforting, and although misdirected, being given a gun alluring.

Fighting begins as civil war breaks out with the brutal slaughter of soldiers, rebels and civilians including innocent women and children. The carnage brings suffering and heartache to the families and friends of the victims, adding sorrow to their already tragic existence.

The war sends the economy into a tailspin as chaos and mayhem prevails. Large parts of the rural areas are controlled by the rebels. International aid goes into decline. Non-government organisations (NGOs) struggle with what is hell on earth, desperately fighting a losing battle, trying to stretch a band-aid over an ever-widening festering chasm (these people are real heroes and deserve a bucketful of medals).

The social conditions that lead to civil war ... must be addressed by the international community.

Rape is rife with both government and rebel soldiers forcing women to give sexual favours in exchange for protection and thereby spreading AIDS (it is estimated that 200,000 women refugees were raped during the genocide in Rwanda).

If all this sounds like a disastrous human catastrophe of gigantic proportions that's because it is. Eventually a ceasefire is negotiated, but it tends to be fragile, mainly because of the lack of trust between the parties.

So What Can Be Done?

The problem—the social conditions that lead to civil war as outlined above—must be addressed by the international community. A feeble attempt was made in the 1990s when under the auspices of the UN [United Nations] the Millennium Development Goals (MDGs) were formulated.

The world leaders came together in September 2000 and here are some examples of what they came up with:

- Halve, between 1990 and 2015, the proportion of people who suffer from hunger

- Reduce by two thirds, between 1990 and 2015, the under five [years of age] mortality rate

- Halve, by 2015, the proportion of people without sustainable access to safe drinking water and basic sanitation.

This is a pathetic attempt at addressing the problem one billion people face every day of their lives. It's like saying to the victims of the [2005] Asian Tsunami or Hurricane Katrina or the recent earthquake in China (to mention just a few), we might be able to halve your plight or help out a bit in fifteen years' time if we get round to it.

> *The international community ... has a huge role to play in stopping existing civil wars and preventing the outbreak of others.*

The main millennium goal should have been this:

The international leaders will collectively work out an alternative method for war to resolve disputes between nations. By 2005, all differences between countries will be resolved in a civilised manner and war will be eliminated forever.

They could have gone on to say, *All nations will reduce military expenditure by 10% by the year 2005 and a further 20% by 2010 and then it will be reviewed with further reductions being the goal. The money and resources saved will be diverted into assisting the developing countries and other global problems, like climate change.*

Franklin D. Roosevelt put it this way when talking about the four essential human freedoms, "The fourth is freedom from fear, which, translated into world terms, means a worldwide reduction of armaments to such a point and in such a thorough fashion that no nation will be in a position to commit an act of physical aggression against any neighbour anywhere in the world."

The best that can be said about the MDGs is that it brought 147 of the worlds' leaders together. This should be a regular occurrence (say once every three to six months) so that problems facing planet earth can be discussed and solutions found. This is what leadership is all about.

Preventing Future Civil Wars

The international community, through the Bretton Wood Institutions, IMF [International Monetary Fund], World Bank, UN agencies, US Aid, EU [European Union] Commission, NGOs and others, has a huge role to play in stopping existing civil wars and preventing the outbreak of others. At the present time, aid to the developing countries is grossly underfunded and tends to be on an ad hoc basis.

What is needed (apart from more funds) is a template, a comprehensive (say) five year master development plan designed with input from the specialist fields of the international agencies mentioned above, but coordinated by one group (maybe the newly established peace-building commission of the UN?).

From past experiences we have a pretty good idea of which aid works and which doesn't. We have learnt, for example, how Europe recovered after WWII [World War II (1939–1945)] through aid from the US, how China and India recently achieved massive sustained economic growth and why Botswana has a well developed economy and Sierra Leone doesn't, even though they have similar resources.

The comprehensive master development plan should include goals, strategies to achieve targets and cover a wide range of topics. This is the best way to prevent civil wars in the future.

The Burden of Future Population Growth Will Fall Mainly on Developing Nations

Mahfuz R. Chowdhury

Mahfuz R. Chowdhury teaches economics at Long Island University in New York and has published articles on the problems of Bangladesh and other developing economies.

The world's population reached six and a half billion in 2006, and is quickly approaching 7.0 billion [as of August 2008]. It appears to be increasing at a rate of about 6.5 million a month or 78 million a year. From a purely mathematical point of view, at the current growth rate of 1.16 per cent per year, the world's population will double in 60 years. However, it is being projected to grow to 9.0 billion by 2050 (as per the United Nations). If this projection holds, it would be an improvement over an earlier forty-year period (1960 to 2000) during which the population of the world practically doubled, from 3.0 to 6.0 billion.

The key point here is that the world's population keeps growing and will continue to grow unless there is a conscious effort by us to limit its growth, or nature imposes some kind of control (like the recent earthquake in China, or the cyclones and tsunami in South and Southeast Asia).

Modern Agriculture Technology

Social scientists from time to time have pondered over the problem of population growth, and rendered their individual opinions on it. Thomas Malthus, an English economist, gained fame by bringing the problem of population growth to the forefront in 1798. His central argument was that population grows at a geometric rate while food output grows at an arithmetic rate, and that makes food scarcity inevitable.

His theory was later dismissed for promoting pessimism on the ground that it failed to consider technological advances in agriculture and food production.

The world's population keeps growing and will continue to grow unless there is a conscious effort by us to limit its growth, or nature imposes some kind of control.

To be sure, technology has achieved miracles and brought enormous successes in innumerable areas, especially in information technology (IT). In terms of agriculture or food production, the result is also astounding. By applying modern technology with improved seeds, fertilizer, irrigation and machinery, it may now be conceivable that a country like the United States could produce enough food to feed the whole world.

The Threat of Population Growth

But the reality is not only different, it also is quite agonizing. As has been noted in the reports of the United Nations, the World Bank and the World Factbook, there are now over three billion people in the world who live in abject poverty, and a billion or about one third of them continue to suffer from severe starvation and malnutrition.

It should, therefore, be obvious that the burden of population growth basically lies with the poor countries. In developed countries, where the unemployment rate is low and future job opportunities are high, population levels are not growing, and some countries even face shrinking populations. Some of these low-growth countries are trying to encourage their citizens to become more family-oriented and raise more children so that future labour shortages could be averted and their pay-as-you-go social security systems, in which pension supplements are financed by taxes on workers, could be sustained.

However, the situation in developing countries is quite the opposite. There the unemployment rates are extremely high-in some cases as high as 60 per cent—and they don't have enough resources to provide their citizens with even the bare necessities of life such as food, clothing and shelter, let alone creating sufficient job opportunities. Since they can not take care of the people they already have, any increase in population simply brings an extra burden on them. But no matter what, more and more people keep filling up these countries every day, month, and year.

For a country like India, which has a population of 1.15 billion, this means preparing dinner for an extra 50,000 people every single night of the year. And for a poor country like Ethiopia, with a per capita GDP of only $800 a year and a population growth rate of 2.23 per cent, it means over 4,700 additional mouths to feed every day.

Since [developing countries] can not take care of the people they already have, any increase in population simply brings an extra burden on them.

One important factor that plays a key role in population growth is the level of education. The higher the level of education of people, the less [their numbers] tend to grow.

The major reason is that an educated person is apt to delay marriage or having a child until a steady income has been secured. The education levels in the affluent societies being high, their growth rates have fallen. As both parents are often busy with their careers, they have little time or interest in nurturing too many kids. In this regard, education of girls is especially important, argues economist Jeffrey Sachs in his book—*Common Wealth: Economics for a Crowded Planet*, 2008.

The growth rate among educated people in the developing countries has also come down to a considerable extent. But the growth rate among the underprivileged people who continue to constitute a huge majority remains high. Since the poor people have no steady income (some practically live hand to mouth), they customarily want more children as security and support in old age. They usually get married very early and produce children that they can not educate or even support. The great irony is that the children born in such a situation tend to breed more of the same year after year. So the reduction in population growth among educated people in the developing countries is being more than compensated by the increase among the underprivileged.

Naturally, because of their lack of proper resources, population increase in poor countries is seen as a big curse and a serious hindrance to their economic expansion.

It should . . . be obvious that the burden of population growth basically lies with the poor countries.

The Example of Bangladesh

Let us take the example of Bangladesh, the seventh largest country in the world in population. By every measure the country has made improvements in education, healthcare, and most, importantly, achieved a respectable economic growth rate of, on average, 5.0 per cent annually in recent years. Yet, the country's poverty level has not come down, and studies show that in real terms it has gone up.

In addition to the massive corruption in the country, the main reason for this is the high growth rate among its underprivileged population. The country adds about 3.0 million to its population every year, where the density of population is already one of the highest in the world. At the current growth rate of 2.02 per cent, per the World Factbook (a lower growth rate is quoted in other reports) the country's population of 150 million is likely to double in 35 years. This will be very similar to the current U.S. population living within the confines of the state of Wisconsin—a state the size of Bangladesh.

Additionally, Bangladesh is a low lying country, and most of its land mass is close to the sea level. As the sea level rises because of the effect of global warming, it is expected that half of the country will be submerged under water in the next 50 or so years. In fact, not only Bangladesh, the fate of many other low lying but heavily populated areas or countries of the world like Bangladesh will be the same when the sea level rises. Now, imagine the inevitable crisis such a situation would create! . . .

Naturally, because of their lack of proper resources, population increase in poor countries is seen as a big curse and a serious hindrance to their economic expansion.

China's One-Child Policy

The challenge of population growth is not imaginary but real for developing countries. In fact, the prospect of their achieving meaningful economic expansion seems to hinge, in great part, on their ability to limit population growth, especially among the underprivileged. Realizing this fact well, China has taken the most drastic measure—restricting the number of children per family to just one. China is in a unique situation to adopt such a policy. Even though it has embraced a capitalist economy, its Communist Party continues to exercise total control over government policy. On the other hand, China has effectively instituted a social security system for the elderly. As a result of China's population policy, the country is soon expected to slip down to the second place in population after India.

However, social scientists are worried that China's one-child policy might also create a serious population imbalance between men and women since most parents prefer a male child over a female child, which, by the way, is still a common phenomenon in developing countries. Currently 119 boys are born in China for every 100 girls. Much of this is the result of the one-child policy and the availability of technology that enables the determination of the sex of the fetus and the availability of selective abortion. There are apparently 18 million more males of marriage age than females, and so the continual increase in the shortfall of women will only lead to increases in social unrest, sex crimes, prostitution, etc. Jeffrey Sachs, in his aforementioned book, emphasizes that state investment in the education of girls can reduce parental bias against female children.

Nevertheless, for traditional societies like Bangladesh, India, Indonesia and Pakistan (some of the most populous countries in the world), where neither a viable social security system nor a strong authoritarian government exists, the Chinese policy of one-child per family would be hard to implement. The biggest hurdle these countries would invariably face is the wrath of religious fundamentalists. Less educated people are easily manipulated or swayed in the name of religion. The argument that children are the gift of God and are cared for by God is still being embraced by too many underprivileged people of the world. It will not be easy to change these attitudes.

India had once tried to restrict its population growth through legislation, but had to abandon the policy under tremendous pressure. Yet, some of the countries are now openly discussing and weighing the policy that China has adopted—one-child per family. In a recent meeting of the Bangladesh Population Council, the local experts have, in fact, recommended precisely such a policy for Bangladesh.

Minimal but Essential Measures

To meet the challenge of population growth in developing countries, in the absence of a China-style mandate of one-child per family, here are some minimal but essential measures that should be considered for immediate implementation: 1) establishing some kind of social security system for the elderly, 2) mandating a minimum age for marriage, 3) discouraging people from getting married or having a child without a steady income, and most importantly, 4) requiring every woman to attend a prescribed class on sexuality, health, hygiene, child bearing, family planning, and birth control before marriage.

In developed countries, girls routinely get lessons on many of these issues by the time they finish junior high school, whereas in developing countries no such formal education is provided to even the prospective wives or mothers. Such knowledge helps a likely mother's role in the decision-making process of raising children. Fertility rates decline when parents feel assured that their children will survive and thrive.

The proposed lessons for women before marriage might consist of just a simple video presentation with a question-and-answer session. Considering the poverty level of the people in developing countries, special emphasis should be given on inexpensive and relatively safe methods of birth control like the timely withdrawal method (medically described as coitus interruptus). This form of birth control might even be more acceptable to religious leaders.

In any case, educating women as well as men on the implications of their actions or inaction on family matters would be the best way to achieve not only the desired goal of population stabilization but also basic healthcare of the child, which most developing countries are clearly striving to achieve. Considering all the consequences, developing countries could ill afford not to confront the population problem head-on.

Global Warming Threatens to Deepen Poverty in the Developing World

Elizabeth K. Gardner

Elizabeth K. Gardner is a writer for Purdue University News, which handles press releases related to university research and other matters.

Urban workers could suffer most from climate change as the cost of food drives them into poverty, according to a new study that quantifies the effects of climate on the world's poor populations.

A team led by Purdue University researchers examined the potential economic influence of adverse climate events, such as heat waves, drought and heavy rains, on those in 16 developing countries. Urban workers in Bangladesh, Mexico and Zambia were found to be the most at risk.

"Extreme weather affects agricultural productivity and can raise the price of staple foods, such as grains, that are important to poor households in developing countries," said Noah Diffenbaugh, the associate professor of earth and atmospheric sciences and interim director of Purdue's Climate Change Research Center who co-led the study. "Studies have shown global warming will likely increase the frequency and intensity of heat waves, drought and floods in many areas. It is important to understand which socioeconomic groups and countries could see changes in poverty rates in order to make informed policy decisions."

The team used data from the late 20th century and projections for the late 21st century to develop a framework that examined extreme climate events, comparable shocks to grain production and the impact on the number of impoverished people in each country.

Thomas Hertel, a distinguished professor of agricultural economics and co-leader of the study, said that although urban workers only contribute modestly to total poverty rates in the sample countries, they are the most vulnerable group to changes in grains production.

"Food is a major expenditure for the poor and, while those who work in agriculture would have some benefit from higher grains prices, the urban poor would only get the negative effects," said Hertel, who also is executive director of Purdue's Center for Global Trade Analysis. "This is an important finding given that the United Nations projects a continuing shift in population concentrations from rural to urban areas in virtually all of these developing countries."

With nearly 1 billion of the world's poor living on less than $1 a day, extreme events can have a devastating impact, he said.

Although urban workers only contribute modestly to total poverty rates in . . . [developing] countries, they are the most vulnerable group to changes in grains production.

"Bangladesh, Mexico and Zambia showed the greatest percentage of the population entering poverty in the wake of extreme drought, with an additional 1.4 percent, 1.8 percent and 4.6 percent of their populations being impoverished by future climate extremes, respectively," Hertel said. "This translates to an additional 1.8 million people impoverished per country for Bangladesh and Mexico and an additional half million people in Zambia."

The Research

A paper detailing the work will be published in Thursday's (Aug. 20 [2009]) issue of *Environmental Research Letters*. In addition to Diffenbaugh and Hertel, Syud Amer Ahmed, a recent Purdue [University] graduate and a member of the development research group for The World Bank, co-authored the paper. The World Bank's Trust Fund for Environmentally and Socially Sustainable Development funded the research.

> *With nearly 1 billion of the world's poor living on less than $1 a day, extreme [climatic] events can have a devastating impact.*

The team identified the maximum rainfall, drought and heat wave for the 30-year periods of 1971–2000 and 2071–2100 and then compared the maximums for the two time periods.

The global climate model experiments developed by the Intergovernmental Panel on Climate Change, or IPCC, were used for the future projections of extreme events. The team used an IPCC scenario that has greenhouse gas emissions continuing to follow the current trend, Diffenbaugh said.

"The occurrence and magnitude of what are currently the 30-year-maximum values for wet, dry and hot extremes are projected to substantially increase for much of the world," he said. "Heat waves and drought in the Mediterranean showed a potential 2700 percent and 800 percent increase in occurrence, respectively, and extreme rainfall in Southeast Asia was projected to potentially increase by 900 percent."

In addition, Southeast Asia showed a projected 40 percent increase in the magnitude of the worst rainfall; central Africa showed a projected 1000 percent increase in the magnitude of the worst heat wave; and the Mediterranean showed a projected 60 percent increase in the worst drought.

A statistical analysis was used to determine grain productivity shocks that would correspond in magnitude to the climate extremes, and then the economic impact of the supply shock was determined. Future predicted extreme climate events were compared to historical agricultural productivity extremes in order to assess the likely impact on agricultural production, prices and wages. Because the projected changes in extreme rainfall and heat wave events were too large for the current model to accept, only the extreme drought events were incorporated into the economic projections, making the projected poverty impacts a conservative estimate, he said.

Bangladesh, Mexico and Zambia showed the greatest percentage of the population entering poverty in the wake of extreme drought.

To assess the potential economic impact of a given change in wages and grains prices, the team used data from each country's household survey. The estimates of likely wage and price changes following an extreme climate event were obtained from a global trade model, called the Global Trade Analysis Project, or GTAP, which is maintained by Purdue's agricultural economics department.

Purdue's GTAP framework is supported by an international consortium of 27 national and international agencies and is used by a network of 6,500 researchers in 140 countries.

Large reductions in grains productivity due to extreme climate events are supported by historical data. In 1991 grains productivity in Malawi and Zambia declined by about 50 percent when southern Africa experienced a severe drought.

Diffenbaugh said this is an initial quantification of how poverty is tied to climate fluctuations, and the team is working to improve the modeling and analysis system in order to enable more comprehensive assessments of the link between climate volatility and poverty vulnerability.

CHAPTER 2

Did the Global Financial Crisis Hurt Developing Nations?

Chapter Preface

When the recession hit the United States in 2007, China, along with other countries, worried about its global effects. As the world's fastest developing country, China feared that the recession might put the brakes on its phenomenal economic growth—success that had resulted from economic reforms adopted after 1978 and that had transformed China from a backward nation into the world's second-largest economy, after the United States. In just a few decades, Chinese economic development lifted hundreds of millions of people out of poverty, improved health and infant mortality, and dramatically raised the country's standard of living. But China's fears of a slowdown were soon realized, as the recession spread around the world. Effects in China included a reduced demand for Chinese exports, drops in housing prices, and losses in other industrial sectors such as electricity production, textiles, and information technology—signs that the country's economic growth was slowing. A Chinese economy that had been reliably growing at a rate of more than 10 percent each year suddenly slowed to about 6 percent in late 2008. Fortunately, however, China was able to avoid some of the worst devastation from the recession due to its conservative financial policies, and the Chinese government acted quickly to stem the damage to its economy.

Unlike the United States and many other Western nations, China escaped much of the financial sector damage caused by the downfall of large financial institutions that held toxic mortgage-related securities called derivatives. This is because China's financial institutions do not trade much in derivatives. Although some of China's large, government-owned banks did experience losses, because they were creditors of the Wall Street investment firm Lehman Brothers, these losses were not large enough to bring down China's financial sector.

With its financial institutions intact, China's main response to the economic crisis was a huge $586 billion stimulus package announced on November 10, 2008. The stimulus, described by some commentators as the biggest stimulus program in global history, sought to encourage domestic consumption and growth in ten areas: housing, rural infrastructure, transportation, health and education, environment, industry, disaster rebuilding, incomes, taxes, and finance. The package included classic stimulus elements—tax breaks and increased government spending for new infrastructure, combined with lowered interest rates to loosen credit. The emphasis on infrastructure helped cement, iron, and steel producers. The easy credit policies jump-started major projects to help rural areas, aided a variety of small and large businesses, and encouraged Chinese consumers to spend more freely. The government also chose not to devalue its currency, the yuan, during the recession. For many years the yuan had been tied to the US dollar, but this was changed in 2005, when the Chinese decided to let it float above the value of the dollar. Although other nations have complained about this policy, it helps to boost Chinese exports—important during the recession.

Observers credit China's aggressive stimulus and fiscal response with sparking renewed growth by the second half of 2009. By the end of 2009, economic growth had surged to 8.7 percent, with the fourth quarter of that year registering a growth rate of 10.7 percent. In 2010, the Chinese economy continued to achieve a double-digit growth rate of 10.3 percent, thanks in part to a rapid growth spurt of 11.9 percent in the first quarter of 2010. China, along with several other countries, including India, Brazil, and Canada, were the biggest successes in the global economic crisis.

In fact, China not only survived the recession; many commentators say the nation actually used the downturn to move its economy forward. As the recession hit, China was extremely well-positioned economically. It had a budget surplus and had been raising interest rates to control its warp-speed growth. This position allowed the Chinese government room to maneuver so that it could pump a great deal of stimulus into its economy when growth was needed most. In addition, the Chinese chose to invest in areas that would yield significant returns in future growth—such as massive investments in infrastructure and new energy technologies. China spent much of the last decade building up its cities, and now it is directing investment toward rural areas. For example, China plans to spend $200 billion on railways, much of it on high-speed rail, and build forty-four thousand miles of new roads and a hundred new airports in order to link rural areas with urban centers. China also is investing in its energy future, spending far more on solar, wind, and battery technologies than has the United States.

Some analysts suggest that China's economy could become overheated as a result of these government investments, possibly leading to inflation or a housing bubble similar to the one that started the US recessionary spiral; however, other experts believe that the fundamental pillars of China's economy are strong and that the Chinese leaders, who are not required to work through a democratically elected Congress as is the US government, are able to exercise tight control over the rate of economic growth. As a result, China's economy is expected by many to continue on a path of sustained and steady growth.

Many other developing countries, however, experienced great suffering as a result of the global financial crisis. The authors of the viewpoints in this chapter explain how the economic recession affected various parts of the developing world.

Developing Nations Have Been Hard-Hit by the Global Financial Crisis

Diana Alarcon, Stephany Griffith-Jones, and José Antonio Ocampo

Diana Alarcon is a senior advisor for the Bureau for Development Policy at the United Nations Development Programme (UNDP), which strives to reduce poverty, increase literacy, and create jobs in nonindustrialized nations. Stephany Griffith-Jones is a professor and researcher, as well as the executive director of the Initiative for Policy Dialogue at Columbia University. José Antonio Ocampo is a professor and the director of economic and political development concentration at Columbia University.

The global economy is in crisis as a result of inadequate regulation and supervision of banks and financial markets. The prudential regulation and supervision recommended to developing countries was largely ignored in the developed nations. No country, however, is spared from the consequences of the downturn. The impact on developing countries is even greater.

Pain for Developing Countries

The crisis is driven by the reversal of the three factors that fuelled the economic boom of 2003–2007. This period saw exceptional levels of financing (private flows to some countries and overseas development assistance to others), high commodity prices and large flows of remittances. The continuing decline in capital flows and exports is hurting the developing countries, despite their having adhered to stringent macroeconomic frameworks.

Diana Alarcon, Stephany Griffith-Jones, and José Antonio Ocampo, "How Does the Financial Crisis Affect Developing Countries?" *International Policy Centre for Inclusive Growth*, April 2009. www.ipc-undp.org. Copyright © 2009 by International Policy Centre for Inclusive Growth. Reproduced by permission.

The accumulation of international reserves and lower levels of external debt allow some developing countries to protect themselves from the rapid deterioration of capital flows. But the contraction of credit, its high cost and the volatility of portfolio investments have already led to a contraction of financial flows. Bank lending to emerging markets fell from a peak of US$410 billion in 2007 to US$167 billion in 2008, and is projected to fall to US$60 billion in 2009.

The continuing decline in capital flows and exports is hurting the developing countries, despite their having adhered to stringent macroeconomic frameworks.

Lower trade volumes will be the main channel of transmission to exporters of manufactures and services (including tourism). The volatility of commodity prices will also affect exporters of primary goods. In countries like Congo, Equatorial Guinea, Gabon and Nigeria, oil provides more than 50 per cent of government revenues from commodity exports. In Côte d'Ivoire and Guinea, cocoa and minerals account for a fifth of revenues. Cotton and aluminium exports provide a fifth of tax revenues in Tajikistan. In Trinidad and Tobago, and in Bolivia, commodities account for 22 and 12 percent of GDP [gross national product, a measure of a country's total economic output] respectively. The prospects for commodity prices remain poor. Recent projections by the World Bank forecast a 25 per cent reduction in energy prices in 2009 and a 23 per cent fall in non-energy commodity prices.

Remittances often provide a safety net in recipient countries. Income from migrant workers helps stabilise consumption levels when recipient economies contract. But remittances have been falling since 2008 in the range of 1 per cent to 6 per cent.

The decline in remittances will be devastating to countries that largely depend on them. For instance, remittances make up 45 per cent of Tajikistan's GDP. Guyana relies on remittances for a quarter of its income.

What Can Be Done to Help?

What should be done to mitigate the impact of the crisis? In most developing countries, macroeconomic indicators, including the accumulation of reserves, have improved in the last five years.

Those countries are much better placed to adopt expansionary fiscal and monetary policies. Infrastructure investments and social spending on nutrition, basic education and health care are essential. There is also an opportunity to expand non-traditional exports through a mix of exchange rate policies and sectoral incentives.

> *Remittances often provide a safety net in recipient countries ... [but a] decline in remittances will be devastating to countries that largely depend on them.*

Concerted international action is also needed. A new system of financial regulation should be built upon two broad principles: the need to incorporate counter-cyclical mechanisms in order to correct for the boom-bust nature of financial markets; and effective regulation whereby the domain of the regulator is the same as the domain of the market to be regulated, which is global in nature.

Reforms are needed in three areas. First is the creation of a meaningful and truly global reserve currency with a substantial expansion of resources to provide counter-cyclical liquidity to developing countries. Second, with greater voice given to developing countries, the International Monetary Fund (IMF) can be instrumental in coordinating global macroeconomic policy. Third, IMF lending has to come without the overly burdensome conditionality of the past. It must have quick-disbursing facilities for countries with strong economic policies facing temporary liquidity problems.

The Global Recession Has Increased Poverty and Slowed Development in Many Developing Nations

Swati Mylavarapu

Swati Mylavarapu is a consultant with Dalberg Global Development Advisors in San Francisco, California.

The global recession has had remarkably local effects. As hardship hits our own pocketbooks and destabilizes our local communities, people's attention naturally focuses on the recession's impact on them. In America, the recession has been a story of elite Wall Street greed that has cost Main Street Americans their jobs and their homes. In Europe, there has been the added complexity of determining "who will save who." . . . This myopia has meant that little attention is being paid to the recession's effects on developing countries. Over 85% of the world's population lives in these countries. We're talking about what the recession has meant for over 4 out of every 5 people in the world.

The Recession and Developing Nations

If we turn our attention to this part of the world, a problematic trend becomes apparent. The global recession has produced two divergent experiences in the developing nations.

In some BRIC [Brazil, Russia, India, and China] states, the largest economic powers among developing countries, (often rapid) growth continues—if slightly tempered. But the difference between 10% and 7.6% growth rates, experienced in India pre and post-recession, is marginal given that most

Swati Mylavarapu, "Building a More Inclusive Global Financial System," *Global Policy Journal*, May 7, 2010. www.globalpolicyjournal.com. Copyright © 2010 by Swati Mylavarapu. Reproduced by permission.

countries' economies have been shrinking. And to answer [German economic adviser Rainer Breul's blog-posted] question of "who's buying the next round," Brazil, China and Russia are among the top 15 lenders to the US.

China is leading this trend. Thanks in part to a domestic stimulus package equivalent to 6% of GDP [gross domestic product, a measure of a country's wealth] ($660B [billion]) that bolstered China's booming manufacturing industry, the country is on track to become the world's second largest economy by year end [2010]. China faces the relative luxury of managing inflation from rapid growth in a time when most of the world faces deflation. Underlying its growth is comforting liquidity; the central bank has raised reserve requirements for lenders to a whopping 14.5–16.5% (compared to virtually eliminated requirements in the US) in an attempt to slow down lending.

For many [developing nations] in the lower socioeconomic brackets . . . , as well as billions in other poorer countries, poverty has increased and the damage may last a while.

But for many in the lower socioeconomic brackets within the BRICs, as well as billions in other poorer countries, poverty has increased and the damage may last a while. Growth has slowed or stopped in many of these countries. The World Bank estimated that GDP in developing countries would slow to 2.1% in 2009, much lower than the 5.8% average seen in 2008. Even worse, the pool of development financing that was available before the recession has shrunk. The Bank estimates that at least 84 of 109 developing countries across Europe, Central Asian Latin America and Sub-Saharan Africa will face financing gaps.

The recession also threatens longer-term recovery and inclusive growth prospects in these countries. In poorer states, when growth declines by a few percentage points, populations living on the cusp of the poverty line plunge decidedly below it. The number of people living in extreme poverty in these countries has risen. That means, for example, that the proportion of African workers earning less than $2 a day rose nearly 3% to 86.6% in 2009.

Millions of individuals have lost what limited ability they may have had to invest in longer term productive assets, such as business equipment, houses—or a child's education. Basic services such as nutrition and health care have become inaccessible. Even when the recession ends, these individuals will not have the means to bounce back with the rest of the economy.

An Inclusive Global Financial System

During this recession, the mistakes of a wealthy few have caused devastation for a poor majority who can least afford it. If ever there was a case for a more inclusive global financial regime, this is it. So what might such a system include?

> *The recession also threatens longer-term recovery and inclusive growth prospects in [developing] countries.*

Expanding the financial governance system from the G8 [the world's top eight economies] to include 12 other nations was a starting point. Now that forum must be used to create effective sector-wide regulation. Liberalization of the global financial system and accompanying banking deregulation in the 1990s ensured the recession's global spread. As much as developed countries are loathe to admit it, they championed these flawed policies.

Protectionism, which increases during recessions, must be resisted. The US's "buy American" provisions in its economic stimulus package, for instance, exempt other advanced industrial nations and so effectively discriminate against poor ones.

If such measures will continue, we at least need mechanisms to offset the unfair advantage it gives to firms in developed countries.

To create a more equitable and stable system, today's dollar-based reserve system must become a more global one. A UN [United Nations] Commission of Experts has called for such a measure. The current system places a large burden on developing countries, which must set aside huge dollar reserves.

Development aid should be guaranteed in future financial crises. This is perhaps the most controversial proposal. Still, [poverty expert] Joseph Stiglitz goes so far as to argue that 1% of developed country stimulus packages should be mandatorily set aside to help developing countries. In times of hardship, aid is needed even more to avert devastating consequences for the most vulnerable populations.

The era of globalization will not end with this recession. If anything, the rapid spread and globally devastating effects of this crisis underscores just how interdependent the world financial system has become. A global financial system that prevents future crises will only emerge if reforms cater to the needs of a too-often-sidelined majority living in developing countries.

Developing Nations Fear a Second Financial Crisis

Jayati Ghosh

Jayati Ghosh is professor of economics at Jawaharlal Nehru University in India and the executive secretary of International Development Economics Associates (IDEAs). She is also a regular columnist for several journals and newspapers and a member of the National Knowledge Commission, which advises the prime minister of India.

It's been an difficult year globally. [The year 2010] began with much relief and congratulations all round, based on perceptions that the financial crisis had been handled effectively, that the Great Recession was over and that significant economies (especially in the developing world) were powering their way back to rapid growth. But it is ending on a much more tentative and even troubled note.

The rebounding of output barely touched unemployment, which remains at historically high levels in most countries. The sovereign debt problems in Europe are just an indication that the financial crisis is far from over, and will continue to reveal itself in new forms for quite some time to come. Meanwhile, the stingy and (so far, at least) visionless response of the stronger economies to the crises in peripheral Europe has condemned them to intensified contraction and ensured that the EU [European Union] will generate little growth and much instability in the near future.

But those shaking their heads from a distance over difficulties in the eurozone should be considering the other financial problems that continue to fester and will raise their ugly heads soon enough: the persistent depression in housing and real estate markets in the US and other developed and some developing countries, which contributes to asset deflation; the many other bad debts that are piling up quietly, like student loans and consumer credit; the continued incentives for risky behaviour by banks that have benefited from large government support; renewed speculative activity in commodity markets, which has pushed up primary commodity prices to close to their peaks of 2008.

Fears of Developing Nations

For developing countries, this last feature is probably one of the greatest concerns—creating the fear that once again we will witness a global food crisis, driven not so much by real supply and demand factors (which have not changed that much) but by speculative activity causing sharp spikes in oil and food prices that are then transmitted to consumers across the developing world. Regulation that might have controlled this speculation is still being formalised in the US and has yet to be drafted in Europe. Meanwhile, the poor will continue to be battered by rising oil and food prices.

For developing countries, [rising commodity prices are] ... creating the fear that once again we will witness a global food crisis.

Prospects look even gloomier because national economic policy making has shifted from coordination to conflict mode. Loose monetary policies in the US and Europe may have domestic goals in mind, but they contribute to the carry trade that sends hot money to developing countries and pushes up their exchange rates and domestic prices. Since most of them are still obsessed with exports as the engine of growth, they try to resist this. So currency wars have already started, but in a subtle, shadow-boxing way. The gloves are not yet off, but they could be soon, because no one seems sure where the growth is supposed to come from.

For large parts of the world economy, things are going to get worse before they get better. And in places where they are supposedly getting better, they are going to get even more uncertain.

The Financial Crisis Did Not Greatly Harm Many Emerging Economies

Paolo Senatore

Paolo Senatore is head of portfolio management at RMB Private Bank in South Africa.

The sustainability of the rapidly growing emerging market countries Brazil, Russia, India and China known as the BRIC countries (the acronym invented by [US investment firm] Goldman Sachs) has definitely been challenged by the global financial crisis. These economies have weathered this storm much better than some of their developed counterparts. During the economic downturn, the 'flight to safety' resulted in extensive capital outflows from emerging markets.

However, this was a temporary phenomenon, as investors recognized the strengths of these economies evident in their significant growth trajectories, and investment returned with vengeance. The BRIC nations are exiting the global recession at a fast pace underpinned by their strong foreign exchange reserves, high level of household savings and low corporate debt. It is believed that by 2014, these BRIC countries will contribute over half of the world's GDP [gross domestic product, a measure of total economic output] growth.

A Growing China

Further, Goldman Sachs believes that China may well become the world's largest economy by 2030. As the globe recovers from the recession, one wonders whether this is a transformational moment similar to that seen after the Second World

War in which the US arose as a super power leaving behind the debt-laden European countries. China's size coupled with its liberal trade policies has stuck out as the most dominant player of this group of four and is seen by many as the future engine of global economic growth. As a consequence of the global financial crisis, China was forced to amend its previously unsustainable export model, as a result of a decline in US and European spending.

> *The BRIC nations are exiting the global recession at a fast pace underpinned by their strong foreign exchange reserves, high level of household savings and low corporate debt.*

Chinese policy makers acted swiftly to stimulate domestic demand thereby ensuring that they maintain their average annual GDP growth at 8% or higher. Unlike their western counterparts, China was financially able to afford their stimulus package backed by USD2 [US$2] trillion in foreign exchange reserves, huge domestic savings and an almost balanced budget. As the global financial crisis unfolded in 2008, China acted quickly to ease monetary and fiscal policy allowing its economy to benefit from cheaper imported commodities by either purchasing inventories to replace high-cost domestic production or in an effort to stockpile at lower prices.

This Asian economy overtook Germany in 2007 as the third largest economy; in 2009, they became the world's largest exporter of manufactured goods and surpassed the US as the leading global auto market. It has recently been confirmed that China has also overtaken Japan as the 2nd largest economy globally. China's economy expanded by 8.7% in 2009 after returning to double-digit growth in the fourth quarter. Recent economic data have sparked concerns over the surge in inflation during the latter part of last year [2009]. Cheap money has led to asset-price inflation as highlighted by rapidly increasing equity and property market prices. Some market commentators fear that an economic bubble is forming and that this economy may eventually overheat. The People's Bank of China has allayed concerns somewhat by recently tightening monetary policy. Specifically, they have increased the amount its commercial banks are required to hold as reserves. This was after loans in the first two weeks of 2010 reached unprecedented levels.

China and other emerging markets are expected to remain resilient supported by the continued growth of the middle class population within these economies.

Furthermore, there are increasing pressures from international trading partners for the Chinese to abandon the peg of the Renminbi [Chinese currency] to the US dollar and allow its currency to appreciate. After being revalued in 2005, the Renminbi was allowed to appreciate by more than 20% against the US dollar until mid 2008 when the peg was reinstated in an effort to insulate its exports from the financial crisis. However, as Chinese exports rebound, gradual currency reform is largely expected. Sceptics believe that investors should prepare for a perilous ride as risks in China multiply. On the other hand, China has the most attractive prospects in comparison to other emerging markets and is expected to rapidly return to trend growth in the first half of 2010.

Domestic demand in China and other emerging markets are expected to remain resilient supported by the continued growth of the middle class population within these economies. We remain positive on emerging markets as an investment destination considering the growing economic importance that these BRIC countries and specifically the role China has played; exposure to these economies will undoubtedly become an influential part of future offshore investing.

Developing Nations Resisted the Global Recession by Showing Fiscal Prudence

The Economist

The Economist is a weekly political and business newspaper based in Great Britain.

The political and social consequences of the worst economic crisis since the Great Depression have been milder than predicted. In developing countries, at least, governments have not fallen in a heap, as they did after the Asian crisis of 1997–98. They have not battled their own people on the streets, as happened in Europe during the 1930s. Social-protection programmes have survived relatively unscathed. There have been economic-policy shifts, naturally, but no panicky retreat into isolation, populism or foreign adventures. The good news has not been spread evenly, of course: some countries have ridden the storm more successfully than others. And these are only first-round effects: things could still get worse. So far, though, resilience has been the order of the day.

Gloomy Predictions

This was not expected a year ago [at the end of 2008]. Then, it seemed likely that normal rules would apply—that when the rich world sneezes, developing countries get swine flu. In the fourth quarter of 2008, when rich economies were contracting by 5% to 10% a year, real GDP [gross national product, a measure of a country's total economic output] fell at an average annualised rate of around 15% in some of the world's most dynamic economies, including Singapore, South Korea

The Economist, "Counting Their Blessings," December 30, 2009. www.economist.com. Copyright © 2009 by The Economist. Reproduced with permission.

and Brazil. The fall in Taiwan's industrial output—down by a third during 2008—was worse than America's worst annual fall during the Depression.

Emerging markets seemed likely to suffer disproportionately because of their trade and financial links with the West. Exports in that dreadful last quarter of 2008 fell by half in the Asian tigers [an economic alliance among Hong Kong, Singapore, South Korea, and Taiwan] at an annualised rate; capital flows to emerging markets went over a cliff as Western banks "deleveraged". The Institute of International Finance (IIF), a think-tank in Washington, DC, forecast that net private capital flows into poor countries in 2009 would be 72% lower than at their peak in 2007, an unprecedented shrinkage.

During 2009 the largest developing-country stockmarkets recouped most or all of the losses they had suffered during 2008.

As people peered ahead into 2009, no forecast looked too dire. "The end of globalisation" was a common refrain. Some thought emerging markets would turn inward to protect themselves from the contagion of the West. Others forecast that hundreds of millions of people would be tipped into hunger. The IMF's [International Monetary Fund, an internal organization that oversees the global financial system] managing director, Dominique Strauss Kahn, fretted that unless governments did the right things at the right time, there was a "threat of civil unrest, perhaps even of war".

A Healthy Recovery

At the start of 2010 there are indeed a billion hungry people, for the first time in 40 years. But the other forecasts now look excessively gloomy. Whereas the last three months of 2008 saw one disaster after another, the end of 2009 was a period of healthy recovery, as measured by capital, bond and stockmarkets.

During 2009 the largest developing-country stockmarkets recouped most or all of the losses they had suffered during 2008. October 2009 saw the largest monthly inflow into emerging-market bond funds since people started tracking the numbers in 1995. Russia's central bank estimated that the country would attract $20 billion of capital inflows during the fourth quarter, compared with capital outflows of $60 billion in the first nine months. The IIF now reckons that net private capital flows to developing countries will more than double in 2010 to $672 billion (still a long way below their peak). So much new money is flooding into emerging markets that calls for capital controls are echoing around the developing world.

This craze for emerging-market paper could perhaps prove [to be] a bubble. But as a measure of reputational change, it is accurate. Countries that were disaster zones at the start of 2009 achieved gold-rush status by the end of it. This turnaround reflects a resilient economic performance during the recession. It also reflects a stunning degree of political and social cohesion.

The most important economic reason for this is that emerging markets were less affected by the rich world's recession than seemed likely early in 2009. Big populous countries—China, India, Indonesia—did not tip into recession; they merely suffered slower growth. Brazil and the Asian tigers saw output fall but bounced back. The pattern, though, was variable. The Baltic states endured a depression; Mexico suffered from its dependence on America; eastern Europe was harder hit than Asia; poor African countries suffered more than middle-income Asian ones.

Overall, the loss of output in emerging markets during 2007 was somewhat greater than it had been in the Asian crisis of 1997–98, but less than had been expected and much less than the fall in world GDP. Emerging markets benefited from their own economic-stimulus programmes and from policy activism in rich countries. Rich-country bail-outs and monetary loosening stemmed worldwide financial panic and helped stoke an appetite for emerging-market exports and assets. In addition, some developing countries built up big cushions of foreign-exchange reserves after the Asian crisis, which afforded them some protection.

> *Countries that were disaster zones at the start of 2009 achieved gold-rush status by the end of it. This turnaround reflects a resilient economic performance during the recession.*

Surprising Stability

This economic resilience has had big political and social benefits. Politically, the most striking feature of the crisis is how little instability it caused. The worst slump in decades has so far led to the fall of just one emerging-market government: Latvia's (Iceland's government also collapsed). Other east-European governments have come under pressure, notably Hungary's.

But two of the biggest emerging markets—India and Indonesia—held national elections in 2009, and both were won by the ruling party. This was unusual in India, which traditionally votes against incumbents. In another emerging giant, Brazil, the outgoing president is likely to leave office in 2010 with poll ratings in the stratosphere (Luis Inácio Lula da Silva's favourability ratings stayed above 60% for most of 2009). The global crisis seems to have consolidated, not undermined, the popularity of large developing-country governments, presumably because the economic crisis was perceived to have begun elsewhere and been dealt with efficiently.

Contrast that with what happened during the Asian crisis of 1997–98. Widespread rioting in the wake of abrupt devaluation led to the fall of Suharto's 30-year dictatorship in Indonesia. Devaluation added to popular discontent in the Philippines, culminating in the overthrow of President Joseph Estrada. There was mass discontent in Thailand as millions of urban workers lost their jobs and wandered back to their villages. Financial collapse in Russia produced a political crisis and led to the sacking of the prime minister, Sergei Kiriyenko. A couple of years later, Argentina defaulted on its debt and ran through three presidents in ten days at the turn of 2001–02. In country after country, governments reacted to financial stress and plunging currencies by imposing emergency austerity measures which brought them into conflict with rioters on the streets. That has been much rarer this time.

Emerging markets benefited from their own economic-stimulus programmes and from policy activism in rich countries.

The second striking feature of the crisis has been that, with one or two exceptions, it seems not to have caused any fundamental shift of popular opinion. There has been no upsurge of angry pessimism, nor any significant backlash against capitalism or free markets. That doubtless explains much of the political composure.

Compared with people in the West, those in big emerging markets seem in almost a sunny mood. In China, India and Indonesia, according to the Pew Global Attitudes Project in Washington, DC, more than 40% of respondents say they are satisfied with their lives (in China the figure is 87%). In France, Japan and Britain, the share is below 30%. This is unusual: measures of "life satisfaction" tend to rise with income, so you would expect levels to be lower in emerging markets, as they were in 2002–03. The reversal of that pattern may re-flect a sense in those countries of their quick recovery.

It is true that the overall levels hide some disturbing trends. A study of Bangladesh, Indonesia, Jamaica, Kenya and Zambia by the Institute of Development Studies at the University of Sussex found that people there said they were saving less, celebrating together less often and thought that neighbourly support was declining. People also thought children and old people were being abandoned more often. But, overall, such concerns are as great or greater in rich countries.

The mood in emerging markets is both unusual and consequential. To see how, compare what is happening there with trends in parts of the West. Americans, for example, seem to be hankering for isolationism. According to Pew's [Research Center] polling, 49% of Americans now think their country should mind its own business internationally. That is more than 30 points higher than when the question was first asked in 1964. Jim Lindsay of the Council on Foreign Relations points out worrying parallels between what is happening now and America's reaction to the Great Depression, which sparked a period of introspection that ended only with the second world war. Developing countries are not suffering such anger or frustration.

That same resilience informs their attitudes to markets. Arvind Subramanian, of the Petersen Institute for International Economics in Washington, DC, argues that the recession has set off "no serious questioning of the role of the market" in developing countries. It is true that China has seen a disproportionate rise in lending to state-owned enterprises, but this is not necessarily regarded with favour. China's media have been flooded with reports of abuses by state firms, all featuring a newly popular, negative-sounding term *guojin mintui*, which means "the state advances and the private sector retreats".

Asked "Are you better off under free markets?", people in emerging markets are more likely to say yes than those in rich ones. The share of respondents who think they are better off fell in 2009 by between four points (Germany) and ten points (Spain). In most emerging markets, the share either rose (in India and China) or stayed flat (in Brazil and Turkey). No sign of an anticapitalist backlash there.

The combination of political stability and popular composure has given emerging markets what might be called "policy space" in which to act. They have used it to the full—and mostly for the better. This, in turn, has enhanced their reputations for economic management.

Little Big Spenders

At the start of 2009 falls in foreign-trade taxes, remittances, aid, commodity prices and capital inflows all threatened developing countries' fiscal positions, and their social spending especially. For a few, the threat materialised: 20 countries, many in eastern Europe, signed standby arrangements with the IMF and tightened fiscal policy. But by and large, the slash-and-burn approach to crisis management associated with previous bouts of economic trouble was avoided. For the first time in a global recession, emerging markets were free to loosen fiscal policy.

Some produced big stimulus programmes. China's is the best known, but Russia, Hong Kong, Kazakhstan, Malaysia, Vietnam, Thailand, Singapore, Brazil and Chile also unveiled large anti-crisis budgets or counter-cyclical spending programmes. As a share of GDP, stimulus spending by the emerging-market members of the G20 [the 20 most-productive economies] was larger than spending by the rich members. In that sense, emerging markets did more than their Western counterparts to combat global recession. Even countries that could not afford emergency programmes like China's let their fiscal balances deteriorate as counter-cyclical spending got under way. In Africa, oil importers let their budget deficits rise from 2.2% of GDP in 2008 to 6% in 2009.

By ring-fencing social spending, developing countries managed to protect some of their poorest people. Brazil expanded the coverage of its assistance programme for the poor, called Bolsa Familia, by over 1m [1 million] households to 12m. India expanded to the whole country a programme that guarantees 100 days' employment on public works each year to any rural household that wants it. China's massive stimulus programme may have forestalled disaster in the migrant-labour force. Half the 140m labourers working in Chinese cities returned home in early 2009; a fifth stayed there, and another fifth could not find work when they returned to the cities. But as spending on infrastructure started to kick in, employment surged; by the middle of the year, joblessness among rural migrant workers was down to less than 3%. Beyond China, fear of social unrest associated with jobless migrants (as in 1997–98) has not materialised. A forthcoming study of 11 countries by Oxfam, a British NGO [nongovernmental organization], found that migrants took new jobs, often at lower wages or with longer hours. In Vietnam some were even given money to stay in the cities by their families in the countryside—a kind of reverse remittance. But there was no mass return to the villages.

Previous recessions have left most developing countries with their reputations for economic management in tatters. . . . This time, it is the rich whose reputations have been damaged.

Flexibility Is Strength

The Oxfam study describes the myriad ways in which countries resisted the recession. Remittances held up better than expected. Parents refused to take their children out of class, or else switched them from private to public schools.

Some even cut down on their own food to keep children in education. There were outright job losses in some parts of countries' economies, such as export sectors and mining. But the commoner reaction to falling demand was to cut hours and wages, reduce benefits and insist on more flexible working conditions. In other words, the main result of the slow-down was not unemployment (though there was some) but a move towards more flexible labour markets.

How long this can go on is unclear. Cash-transfer and make-work schemes are expensive: most poor countries can-not afford them. Worse, the poorest were more vulnerable than middle-income countries anyway because of the food-price spike of 2007–08: hence the rise in the number of hun-gry people to 1 billion, the highest figure since 1970. In gen-eral, the informal sector (home workers, ragpickers, street vendors) has been hit harder than the formal sector and is be-yond the reach of government anti-poverty programmes. Al-though developing countries have done what they can, it would be wrong to think their people have escaped the reces-sion entirely.

It is worth adding that not all the actions of developing-country governments have been equally enlightened. Emerg-ing markets have been the worst sinners in a new round of protectionism. Whether you look at the number of new trade-damaging measures tracked by the World Trade Organisation, or the numbers of sectors or trading partners hurt, Russia, China and Indonesia are all among the top five protectionists; Argentina is in the top ten. Rich countries have been slightly less destructive. Still, as Simon Evenett, a professor of trade at the University of Saint Gallen, Switzerland, points out, this is not as dreadful as it might have been, or as it was in the 1930s. Only four countries have implemented restrictions af-fecting more than a quarter of their product lines: across-the-board tariff barriers are not the fashion. But as growth picks up and fights for market share increase, these restrictions could lay a basis for further trade disputes.

The Tectonic Consequence

When the Earth's tectonic plates grind against one another, they do not always move smoothly; sometimes they slip. A year after the West's slump began to spread to emerging markets, it has become clear that the recession has been a moment of tectonic slippage, a brief but powerful acceleration in the deep-seated movement of economic power away from rich nations towards emerging markets.

The fiscal response of many emerging markets has enhanced their credibility, and they find themselves with an unexpected reputation for fiscal prudence.

Since 2007, according to [US investment firm] Goldman Sachs, the biggest emerging markets—Brazil, Russia, India and China—have accounted for 45% of global growth, almost twice as much as in 2000–06 and three times as much as in the 1990s. It used to be said that although emerging markets were contributing an expanding share of world growth, they could not claim to be the real engine for the global economy because final demand for their exports lay in America. But that argument is weaker now that China has overtaken America as the main market for the goods of the smaller Asian exporters. The recession showed that economic power is leaching away from the West faster than was thought.

Previous recessions have left most developing countries with their reputations for economic management in tatters, and with credibility to regain in capital markets. This time, it is the rich whose reputations have been damaged. The fiscal response of many emerging markets has enhanced their credibility, and they find themselves with an unexpected reputation for fiscal prudence. The debt-to-GDP ratio of the 20 largest emerging markets is only half that of the top 20 rich nations. Over the next few years rich countries' debt will rise further, so emerging markets' indebtedness will be only one-third of theirs by 2014. Already there are signs that financial markets are rewarding them for good behaviour. Sovereign-risk spreads have been lower in the biggest emerging markets than in some euro-zone countries; in 2009, Hong Kong did more initial-public offerings than New York or London.

At the start of the crisis, a Mexican minister sighed: "At least this time it's not our fault." The comment was laden with sad irony: like everyone else, he expected that Mexico's inno-cence would make no difference and that emerging markets would be hammered anyway. But they have not been. So far the story of global recession in emerging markets has had that rarest of themes: virtue rewarded.

Developing Nations May Recover from the Global Recession Faster than Rich Countries

Arif Anis

Arif Anis is a writer, blogger, personal development coach, and a motivational speaker.

Haves and have-nots; the discord is never ending since time immemorial. Think of all the relevant synonyms in the dictionary. *Underprivileged, deprived, underclass, unfortunates, marginalised* and *the third world*—blah blah blah. These words bring all the images of despondences, misery and wretchedness. Most of us have an idea when we talk about the developing world and its back-breaking load of challenges; i.e., debts, unemployment, crime, quality of life, illiteracy. It is rare when some good news is heard about the developing countries [but] . . . in [these] times of financial Black Death, the developing countries seem to be getting some benefit from the economic downturn. This time the beggars are not the losers. It is not that the developing countries are not going to get hit by the avalanche. They are perhaps more vulnerable but expected to make quicker recovery, as revealed in a recent report.

A Robust Recovery

According to the World Bank Report on the world's financial stability released on 22 March, 2010, global GDP [gross domestic product, a measure of a country's total economic output], which declined by 2.2 percent in 2009, is expected to grow 2.7 percent in 2010 and 3.2 percent in 2011. World trade volumes, which fell by a staggering 14.4 percent in 2009, are projected to expand by 4.3 and 6.2 percent this year [2010] and in 2011, according to the report.

> "The strength of the recovery will depend on consumer and business-sector demand picking up and the pace at which governments withdraw fiscal and monetary stimulus," [But] "if this is done too soon, it might kill the recovery; yet waiting too long might re-inflate some of the bubbles that precipitated the crisis."

It is not that the developing countries are not going to get hit by the avalanche. They are perhaps more vulnerable but expected to make quicker recovery.

The Report predicts that developing countries are expected to make a relatively robust and speedier recovery, with 5.2 percent GDP growth in 2010 and 5.8 percent in 2011—up from 1.2 percent in 2009. Rich countries, which declined by 3.3 percent in 2009, are expected to grow less quickly—by 1.8 and 2.3 percent in 2010 and 2011.

Effects of the recession across the developing world have been varied. United States, Europe and Central Asia have seen the worst of it, while, in contrast, growth continues to be relatively strong in East Asia and the Pacific. South Asia and the Middle East and North Africa have escaped the worst effects of the crisis, while Sub-Saharan Africa has been hard hit, with the outlook for the region remaining uncertain.

Does it augur well for the developing world? Answer is a grim NO. It is still feared that the crises will swamp emerging markets. The developing world and what it has recently achieved are at risk. The developing world is going to face the surge of instability. 1.4 billions people who are surviving on the verge of extreme poverty are mostly in the developing countries. Given the slim margin of survival, the consequences will be much severer in those marginalised areas. Famines, riots, coups, ethnic clashes, gang wars, in short the apocalypse is just around the corner. We have to ensure the costs of the have-nots of the world are kept to the minimum. It was [Karl] Marx who ended his books that became the Communist Manifesto, "Das Kapital" on 'you have nothing to lose except the chains'. Let us all try [to see] that the ravages of financial crises are equally distributed. It is essential if we want to avert the "financial Tsunami" which will wreck the approximately two billion population and then there will be nothing to lose for all of us.

Developing Nations Are Leading the World Economy Back from Recession

Xinhua News Agency

Xinhua News Agency provides online news services in six languages—Chinese, English, Spanish, French, Russian, and Arabic—to people in more than two hundred countries and regions.

The world economy is moving from a post-crisis bounce-back phase of the recovery to slower but solid growth this year [2011] and next year [2012], with developing countries contributing almost half of global growth, according to the Global Economic Prospects 2010, a report released by the World Bank on Wednesday [January 12, 2011].

Developing Countries Lead Recovery

In most developing countries, the GDP [gross domestic product, a measure of a country's total economic output] has regained levels that would have prevailed had there been no boom-bust cycle, noted the report.

"On the upside, strong developing-country domestic demand growth is leading the world economy," said Justin Yifu Lin, the World Bank's chief economist and senior vice president for development economics.

The report contended that [the] East Asia and Pacific region, with GDP growth estimated at 9.3 percent for 2010, led the global recovery. This was on the back of an estimated 10 percent increase in Chinese GDP and a 35 percent increase in its imports.

Xinhua News Agency, "World Bank Says Most Developing Countries Recovered from Crisis, China to Grow 8.7% in 2011," January 13, 2011. Copyright © 2011 by Xinhua News Agency. Reproduced by permission.

The World Bank also said that as the pace of the global re-covery eases, [the] East Asia and Pacific region's growth is projected to slow, but remain strong at 8 percent in 2011 and 7.8 percent in 2012.

The report said [the] global economy, which increased by 3.9 percent in 2010, is expected to grow 3.3 percent this year and 3.6 percent in 2012.

"The world economy is entering into a new phase of re-covery," said Lin.

[The] East Asia and Pacific region . . . led the global recovery.

According to the report, developing countries, which were [the] leading engine of the global recovery after the financial crisis, are expected to grow 7 percent in 2010, 6 percent in 2011 and 6.1 percent in 2012.

They "will continue to outstrip growth in high-income countries, which is projected at 2.8 percent in 2010, 2.4 per-cent in 2011 and 2.7 percent in 2012."

A Strong China

The report predicts China's economy, the biggest emerging economy, is to grow 8.7 percent in 2011 and 8.4 percent in 2012.

"For China, domestic demand contributed some 7.8 per-centage points to overall growth of 10 percent in 2010, with net trade contributing the remainder," said the annual report released by the Washington-based international institution.

The report noted that China's economy is becoming stron-ger to some extent, with industrial output standing some 34 percent above pre-crisis peak levels.

But China's growth moderated over the course of 2010 with domestic demand cooling gradually as stimulus faded and the monetary stance tightened.

The World Bank expects that growth in China is likely to ease from the near 10 percent pace of 2010—due in part to the unwinding of fiscal stimulus, restrictions placed on overheating sectors and a general tightening of monetary conditions in the face of rising inflation pressures.

China remains a source of growth of the global economic recovery and the focal point of regional activity in East Asia.

Nevertheless, industry-led, capital intensive growth is likely to keep GDP gains near 8.5 percent over the period, with net exports contributing smaller shares of growth than in the pre-crisis years.

According to the report, China remains a source of growth of the global economic recovery and the focal point of regional activity in East Asia.

CHAPTER 3

Can Democracy Succeed in Developing Nations?

Chapter Preface

A number of developing nations have overthrown autocratic regimes and held democratic elections in recent decades. One of the most recent examples of a such a movement toward democratic freedoms is Tunisia—a relatively small country in northern Africa bordered by Algeria to the west, Libya to the southeast, and the Mediterranean Sea to the north and east. Once under French colonial rule, Tunisia achieved independence in 1957, adopting a multiparty democratic system of government. Although technically a democracy, Tunisia has become known as one of the world's most autocratic states—a country where one party rules, human rights and freedom of the press are restricted, the Internet is censored, and political corruption is widespread. Tunisians have lived with these types of repression for decades, but this changed with the eruption of spontaneous protests against the government in December 2010. Tunisia's government was overthrown in January 2011, bringing hope for true democracy to the nation.

Tunisia has been controlled since the time of its independence by one political party—the Constitutional Democratic Rally (RCD). Since 1987, the country's president has been Zine El Abidine Ben Ali, a member of the RCD who has gained the reputation as one of the region's most repressive Arab leaders. Under his rule, Tunisia has been politically stable, and wealthy elites have lived well—but only at the expense of the country's poorer citizens, who have suffered from poor living conditions, high unemployment, and a lack of human rights and freedoms. Despite the president's autocratic rule, Tunisia's regime has been supported by the United States, largely because it has prevented the rise of radical Islam among its Arab population and helped Western nations fight against Islamic terrorism.

The uprising in Tunisia—called the Jasmine Revolution after a flower native to the region—began with a series of street protests in December 2010. The protest erupted after Mohamed Bouazizi, an educated computer science graduate who was selling fruit to support his family, was harassed by police and told to pack up his produce cart. Bouazizi threatened to set himself on fire if the local governor did not meet with him, carrying out his threat on December 17, 2010. His suicide produced a martyr for millions of Tunisian youth who had become increasingly frustrated with high unemployment, inflation, and a lack of economic opportunities. Young Tunisians also were disgusted with the country's high-level political corruption made especially visible in 2010 in documents released by Wikileaks, an organization that posts often-secret government information online.

Riots first erupted in Sidi Bouzid, the city where Bouazizi died, organized largely by young Tunisians through Internet sites like Twitter and Facebook. Quickly, however, the protests spread throughout the country and gained support from labor unions, lawyers' groups, and others. The government responded to the unrest with a police crackdown that included beatings and over a hundred deaths, but the unrest continued unabated. President Ben Ali alternately criticized and sought to appease the demonstrators, ordering a government shake-up, closing schools and universities, and promising more jobs. Ultimately, however, he was forced to resign. On January 14, 2011, the president dissolved his government, declared a state of emergency, and fled to Saudi Arabia.

Following the president's departure, a temporary coalition government was created, promising that elections would be held in sixty days. However, protesters rejected the new government, complaining that it contained members of the RCD, and demonstrations continued. On January 27, 2011, Tunisia's prime minister, Mohammed Ghannouchi, announced that six members of the RCD had resigned from the government, meeting protesters' demands. The next chapter of Tunisia's history now must be written and international observers are divided about what might happen. As of early 2011, the country appeared to be in a political vacuum, but it is possible that Tunisia will replace its autocratic system with a much more democratic government. Tunisia has already inspired other political rebellions in the Arab world. In February 2011, Egypt—another Arab country with a long history of repressive rule—experienced widespread protests that forced longtime Egyptian president Hosni Mubarak to resign. Protests also erupted in several other nations in the region, most notably Libya, where leader Muammar al-Gaddafi, who had been in power since a 1969 coup, was killed in October 2011, after an eight-month civil war in the country.

Whether Tunisia will succeed in fully embracing democracy is a question that cannot yet be answered, but democracy does seem to have a broad appeal in many other developing regions as well. The authors of the viewpoints in this chapter address the issue of whether democracy can succeed in the developing world.

Democracy Is the Most Legitimate Form of Government for Developing Nations

Marc F. Plattner

Marc F. Plattner is founding coeditor of the Journal of Democracy *and director of the International Forum for Democratic Studies at the National Endowment for Democracy. He is the author of the 2008 book* Democracy Without Borders? Global Challenges to Liberal Democracy.

The first decade of the twenty-first century has not been a happy time for the fortunes of democracy in the world. After a period of extraordinary advances in the final quarter of the twentieth century, the overall spread of democracy came to a halt, and there have even been signs that an erosion of democracy might be getting underway. According to Freedom House's annual survey [of global civil rights and liberties], there have now been modest declines in the level of freedom in the world for three consecutive years. Earlier in the decade, democratic hopes had been inspired by the success of the "color revolutions" in Serbia, Georgia, Ukraine, and even Kyrgyzstan, but subsequent developments in these countries have on the whole been disappointing. Moreover, nondemocratic regimes elsewhere became obsessed with the threat of color revolutions, and having learned from the failures of their fellow autocrats, they launched a set of efforts that have reduced the space for opposition and civil society groups in their own countries—a phenomenon described as the "backlash" or "pushback" against democracy.

Marc F. Plattner, "Populism, Pluralism, and Liberal Democracy," *Journal of Democracy*, January 2010, vol. 21, no. 1. Copyright © 2010 by Johns Hopkins University Press. Reproduced by permission.

Another indicator of what Larry Diamond [a fellow at the conservative Hoover Institution] has labeled a "democratic recession" is that the world's autocratic regimes have begun to show a new *élan* [enthusiasm] leading other commentators to speak of the emergence of an "authoritarian capitalist" alternative to democracy. In the 1990s, political scientists tended to regard authoritarian regimes as transitory, and studied them largely from the perspective of their potential for achieving progress toward democracy. Of late, however, impressed by the staying power of many of these regimes, scholars have begun to focus on what has enabled them to persist and often to display a considerable degree of stability—a phenomenon that Andrew J. Nathan [a political science professor at Columbia University], writing about China, has dubbed "authoritarian resilience." There is no question that a large number of other nondemocratic regimes, especially in the Middle East and the former Soviet Union, have demonstrated an impressive ability to maintain their hold on power, and it makes good sense to explore the sources of their survival.

The new focus on the resilience of authoritarianism may have led to a tendency to neglect or undervalue the resilience of democracy.

The Resilience of Democracy

At the same time, however, the new focus on the resilience of authoritarianism may have led to a tendency to neglect or undervalue the resilience of democracy—a subject that I believe merits fresh attention. Despite the obstacles that democracy has encountered in recent years, it in fact continues to endure remarkably well. In the first place, in a departure from previous cycles, the "third wave" of democratization that began in 1974 has not yet given way to a third "reverse wave." in which the number of countries experiencing democratic breakdowns substantially exceeds the number giving birth to new democracies. It is true, as Larry Diamond has noted, that the incidence of democratic breakdown or backsliding has increased in the last few years, but the democratic regimes that have succumbed have all been of fairly recent vintage. Put differently, no well-established or consolidated democracies have been lost. In particular, in countries that have achieved high levels of per capita GDP [gross domestic product, a measure of a country's total economic output] there still has not been a single case of democratic breakdown.

Despite the obstacles that democracy has encountered in recent years, it in fact continues to endure remarkably well.

Part of the explanation, of course, is that democratic regimes today enjoy a high degree of legitimacy, not only among their own citizens but in the world at large. This can be seen in the endorsement that democracy has been given by international and regional organizations, in the way in which non-democratic countries try to claim the mantle of democracy for themselves, and in the support for democracy that public-opinion surveys find in every region of the world. As [Indian economist] Amartya Sen has written,

> In any age and social climate, there are some sweeping beliefs that seem to command respect as a kind of general rule—like a "default" setting in a computer program: they are considered right *unless* their claim is somehow precisely negated. While democracy is not yet universally practiced, nor indeed universally accepted, in the general climate of world opinion, democratic governance has now achieved the status of being taken to be generally right.

The high degree of legitimacy that democracy enjoys can also be observed in the paucity of support in established democracies for antidemocratic movements and regimes elsewhere. During the twentieth century, there were significant sources of support in Western public opinion, especially among academics and intellectuals, not only for Marxism, but for [Joseph] Stalin's Soviet Union, for Mao [Zedong]'s China, for [Fidel] Castro's Cuba, and for the [socialist political party] Sandinistas' Nicaragua. In the democratic world today, open backing for the regimes of Russia, China, or Iran is rarely to be found. There is of course, a great deal of criticism of Western and especially U.S. policy toward these regimes, but that is a very different matter from endorsing their ideological claims.

Yet although explicit sympathy for antidemocratic alternatives is virtually absent among significant groups of citizens in consolidated democracies, this cannot be taken to reflect widespread satisfaction on their part with political life in their own countries. When viewed from the vantage point of emerging democracies, the advanced democracies may appear to be paragons of successful governance, but that is not generally how it looks from the inside, where dissatisfaction with politics is widespread. This manifests itself in contempt for politicians (especially the people's chosen representatives in the legislature), frequent outbreaks of scandal and corruption, and declining trust in political institutions. Moreover, across the political spectrum, at least in the United States, one hears heightened expressions of concern about escalating partisanship, a coarsening of political discourse, an inability to get things accomplished, and a broader cultural decline.

Democratic regimes today enjoy a high degree of legitimacy, not only among their own citizens but in the world at large.

It would be hard to deny that many of these complaints have a good deal of justification. Yet in the developed world democracy remains, if not exactly robust, seemingly impregnable. This may in part be due to an increasing acceptance of what has been dubbed "the Churchill hypothesis"—that "democracy is the worst form of Government except for all those other forms that have been tried from time to time." It is surely true that the failures and drawbacks of other types of regimes help to shore up the continuing appeal of democracy. Even cases such as the People's Republic of China, with its remarkable success over the past three decades in achieving economic growth and military power, have not been able to convince citizens in the advanced democracies that they would want to sacrifice their liberties to enjoy the putative benefits of single-party rule. The direction of migration in the world remains overwhelmingly from less free countries to freer ones.

Democracy Will Meet the Challenges of Authoritarian Regimes

Carl Gershman

Carl Gershman is president of the National Endowment for Democracy, a private, congressionally-supported grantmaking institution with a mission to strengthen democratic institutions around the world through nongovernmental efforts.

I've been given 600 seconds to talk about the future of democracy in the whole world. So I'm warning you from the beginning I'm going to be speaking in a little bit of short hand. A lot of people think that democracy has been backsliding in the last ten years. I'll make several arguments to demonstrate why I don't think that has happened and why we may even be at a point today where democracy can make some new gains. I might note, by the way—just admit to you right from the beginning—that I'm a glass-half-full kind of person. That's because of what I do. I help people fight for democracy, and you can't fight for democracy unless you have hope that maybe something is possible, but we also have to be realistic. And there I think it's fair to see the glass as half full.

Hope for Democracy

We speak in Portugal where the "third wave" of democratization began 35 years ago, peaking in the late 1980s and early 1990s. The number of countries designated as "free" in the Freedom House Annual Survey doubled during this period, from 44 to 88, and the total number of democracies, meaning countries rated as electoral democracies or better, grew to about 120. Those numbers have stayed fairly steady. Democracy has certainly lost its forward momentum and it faces stiffer resistance today, but overall the third wave has not given up its gains. The number of "free" countries in the Freedom House survey grew from 86 to 89 during the decade ending in 2008. The number of "partly free" countries grew from 58 to 62. And the number of "not free" countries declined from 48 to 42. So, that's the first point—democracy has not been backsliding in the way some people think it has.

Democracy has certainly lost its forward momentum and it faces stiffer resistance today, but overall the third wave has not given up its gains.

The second point is that public opinion around the world—and this is something that was mentioned briefly in Marc Plattner's paper—is overwhelmingly for democracy. That is true even in countries where democracy has not delivered as some people had hoped it might. The basis for this sustained support was spelled out in the lecture given at the founding of the World Movement for Democracy ten years ago by [Indian economist] Amartya Sen. People favor democracy, he said, for many reasons. One was mentioned a number of times at this conference—that democracy serves the instrumental purpose of advancing peace. Evidence also points to other instrumental purposes—it can create a legal and political environment conducive to economic development and also encourages elected governments, if they're to retain popular support, to respond to the needs of their people through social expenditures for education and health. It also serves the protective function of giving people a way to defend their human rights. Another protective dimension of democracy, famously pointed out by Sen, is that famines have never occurred in countries that are democratic and have a free media. In addition, you can't really fight corruption without democracy, so that's another protective function. All of these purposes explain why democracy is especially important to the common people in countries around the world, since it offers ways for the poor to mobilize to protect their interests. And finally, of course, democracy has an intrinsic value since it is based on the idea that people have rights and dignity. And so it continues to have popular support.

Challenges for Democracy

Finally, and more importantly, I want to discuss the challenges that democracy faces today around the world and why I think it is able to meet those challenges. In each region of the world, democracy is under attack in one way or another. We've talked a lot at this conference about how Russia is behaving in a much more aggressive way in what it calls "the near abroad" and that it also continues to crack down on civil society and independent media. China is a growing economic power, and it is asserting that power not just in Asia but in other regions around the world. There is the rise of radical Islamism that poses a threat to democracy. In Africa there are so many challenges, from the problems of violence and corruption to state failure in Somalia and some other countries. And in Latin America, we've heard a lot of about [Venezuela's president, Hugo] Chávez and [Cuban leader Fidel] Castro, and the rise of populism. But in all these situations, I want to suggest to you, that the authoritarians have their own problems. They have their own vulnerabilities and must contend with movements from below that are pressing for greater democracy. The question is whether these two factors—the vulnerabilities of the authoritarian governments and the pressure coming from below—can lead to democratic breakthroughs? I am not speaking in the short-term, though. I am speaking in generational terms. Let me quickly review each one of these challenges that I mentioned to you.

First Russia. It is a large and relatively strong country. It has nuclear weapons. It has oil. But Russia is also a dysfunctional country. Its economy does not work aside from the production oil, and it's got a demographic crisis that is existential. A recent study by [American historian] Walter Laqueur notes that Russia's population is shrinking annually by 2 percent and that in 50 years it will be a third of its present size. The fact that the Muslim minority in Russia is growing only compounds this existential crisis. Russia also faces a counter-challenge coming from the European Union and its new members from Central Europe and the Baltics that were once part of the Soviet Bloc, especially Poland which is quietly pursuing with its eastern neighbors a counter to the Russian strategy in the near abroad, building an expanding association of new democracies looking toward and linked to Europe and the United States.

Second, China. Yes, China has growing economic influence, but it is not as stable as it might appear. I refer you to a lecture that was given just last month [May 2010] in [China's capital city] Beijing by Yu Jianrong, who directs the Rural Development Institute at the Chinese Academy of Social Sciences. It was an important lecture, given at the Lanshan Forum, where he reached very pessimistic conclusions about the future of China. He characterized China as a country that has rigid stability and lacks mechanisms to resolve problems like the denial of land rights for peasants, the nonpayment of wages for workers, the abuse of homeowner rights of urban dwellers, and the denial of minority rights of Tibetans and Uighurs. Every time one of these groups protests and tries to defend its basic interests, this is seen as a threat to the survival of the state. In this regard, Yu characterizes Chinese thinking as entirely black and white. There is no ability to find a middle ground where conflicts can be negotiated and social problems can be resolved. And so he says that China has only a "rigid stability" which makes it very brittle, not a "resilient stability" that he associates with democracy. India has this resilience, and I suggest to you that in the long run India constitutes a much more viable model for developing countries than China and is inherently a much more stable country, because it is able to adapt to change and withstand inevitable crises.

The authoritarians have their own problems. They have their own vulnerabilities and must contend with movements from below that are pressing for greater democracy.

Third, Islamism. I am not going to go into a very long discussion of Islamism here, but I want [to] refer you to an article that appeared just this week [the last week of June 2010] in the *Wall Street Journal* by our friend Saad Eddin Ibrahim, the leading dissident in Egypt, who spoke about a new Middle East "spring of freedom." He referred to gains or potential breakthroughs in four countries: Kuwait, where four women were elected to parliament; Lebanon, where Hezbollah was set back in the elections earlier this month; Iran, where the Green Revolution is far from defeated; and Turkey, where a party with Islamist roots presides over a stable democracy. He might also have mentioned Indonesia, the largest Muslim country in the world and a stable democracy, something that the forthcoming elections are likely to confirm; India, where the largest Muslim minority in the world, some 140–150 million people, recently helped the Congress party win a resounding electoral victory; Morocco, where the Islamists suffered an important setback in the 2007 elections; and Pakistan, where the Islamists were marginalized in the elections last year. One could go on, but the political threat of Islam is not as severe as some people have feared, even if the terrorist threat remains dire.

Regarding Africa, the problems are grave, as I have noted. But I think we were given . . . today a glimpse of a different African reality by the Rector of the Catholic University of

Mozambique, who told a remarkable story of national rebirth after a period of devastating conflict. The point is that Mozambique is not an isolated case. When the NED [National Endowment for Democracy, a private group that seeks to strengthen democratic institutions] was founded 25 years ago there were three African democracies representing just 3 million people—Botswana, Mauritius, and Gambia. Gambia is no longer a democracy, but today, half of the countries in sub-Saharan Africa are either liberal or electoral democracies. The principal reason for these gains, as we heard . . . today, is that Africa has a vigorous civil society consisting of educational institutions, women's and civic education organizations, think tanks, bar associations, trade unions, student associations, youth groups, religious bodies, electoral monitoring networks, developmental and pro-environmental groups, journalists, community radio broadcasters, groups working on religious and ethnic conflict, and finally, human rights defenders all over the continent. Because of time, I won't speak further about these groups, but they're the reason Africa has made democratic progress that was simply unimaginable in 1990.

And, finally, Latin America. To be sure, Chávez is acting like things are going his way, but Venezuela has the highest inflation in Latin America, it has severe problems of unemployment and a catastrophic crime wave. In fact, Chávez is really on the defensive and trying desperately to hold on. I recently met with Antonio Ledezma, the mayor of Caracas. Not long after his election last November [2009], Chavez passed a law taking away all of his power. This is being contested right now, but I think it shows that Venezuela is a country that is ripe for its own colored revolution, though the struggle will be hard and bitter. Even in Cuba there is now, for the first time, a mass popular movement of opposition at the grassroots. There is a group that monitors actions of civic resistance in Cuba. When they started monitoring such actions in the late 90s, they were able to identify 44 protests. Today they report on over 3,000 of them every year, especially in the center and eastern parts of the island where the population is worse off than in Havana and mostly Afro-Cuban. I could go on at length about this, but let me just note that earlier this week we honored five of these activists, three of whom are in prison, and one of them was able to be linked up by phone to us. We were meeting in the U.S. Congress, and he spoke to us loudly and fearlessly about the struggle he and his comrades are waging. This couldn't have happened 10 years ago, and it is one more example of an autocratic regime with serious vulnerabilities and facing popular movements from below.

China Will Not Gain Respect Until It Embraces Democratic Freedoms

Kwame Anthony Appiah

Kwame Anthony Appiah is a professor of philosophy at Princeton University and author of the 2010 book The Honor Code: How Moral Revolutions Happen.

Liu Xiaobo is a brave man who loves his country. It was an honor to have been among those to nominate him for the Nobel Peace Prize. It's a great thrill that he got it. Now we have to hope that this moment becomes another stepping stone on China's long march toward greater freedom.

China's Voice for Human Rights

This is a crucial moment in China's history, as the Norwegian Nobel Committee clearly understands. Liu rightly wants to underline how far his country has to go to secure the basic democratic freedoms of speech and association. But we also need to remember how far it has come. In the 1960s and 1970s, during the Cultural Revolution [a movement designed to purge capitalism and advance socialism in China in 1966–1976], a whole generation of intellectuals was uprooted. Millions were displaced. The situation today is very different in ways both heartening and discouraging. Now we can identify somewhere between 40 and 50 writers and bloggers whom the Chinese state has imprisoned simply for peacefully speaking their mind.

Of course, the number of those incarcerated represents a tiny fraction of those silenced by their example. A vast apparatus of government censorship—the "Great Firewall"—

remains in place. We have to work to support those in the regime who can already see that this is not only wrong, but also counterproductive. Human rights are everybody's business. And we can't have the productive dialogue with China that it wants—and the world needs—if its government is abusing its own people. We outside need to hear all of China's voices, just as the Chinese do.

As we honor and celebrate Liu's more than two decades of peaceful work for human rights in China, though, he wouldn't want us to forget that he is one among many. One of his many achievements was to participate in the creation of Charter 08, a document outlining the changes China needs to make if it is to become a real democracy. More than 10,000 people have signed this document in the last two years, despite the fact that Liu and many others of the 300-plus original signers have been arrested or harassed by the police.

Human rights are everybody's business.

And then there are people like Gao Zhisheng, the army veteran and human rights lawyer who hasn't been seen since this April [2010]. Gao—whose struggle to achieve an education began in a cave in Shaanxi province, where he was born to a peasant family—has been tortured and imprisoned in the past. And all because he has learned the law, committing great volumes of the Chinese legal code to his formidable memory, and used it to fight corrupt officials and the suppression of religious minorities. While we celebrate Liu, let's also ask the Chinese government where Gao is and what has happened to him.

Or take Chen Guangcheng, another self-taught lawyer. Chen is blind, but he too has used the courts to defend the rights of ordinary rural people. He didn't learn to read until he was in his 20s. But once he did, he filed a lawsuit drawing attention to the suffering of women forced into abortions by officials in Linyi county in Shandong province. So he, too, has been imprisoned. He was released after a four-year sentence just a month ago. Naturally, he is still under surveillance. Let's make sure he also gets our support.

Supporting Democracy

We need to help the Chinese government to see that these people are not, as the regime's spokesmen keep insisting, ordinary criminals, but national treasures. They are seeking to give voice to the aspirations of millions of people. We need to help the Chinese Communist Party understand what it took a long history of struggle for us to learn in the Western world: A government that cannot hear from its people cannot govern well. My friend Amartya Sen, an economics Nobel laureate, has shown, in essence, that famines don't occur in democracies. A government that hears its people can serve them better. Democracy makes some things more difficult—but mostly they're things, like corruption and the abuse of human rights, that *ought* to be difficult.

> *We need to help the Chinese Communist Party understand . . . [that] a government that cannot hear from its people cannot govern well.*

There's actually a long history of outsiders helping China's leaders make moral advances. In the late 19th century, many among the literati who governed the country were persuaded to abandon the 1,000 year old practice of foot-binding, in part through a productive dialogue with Protestant missionary critics. That dialogue worked, I believe, because the critics took the trouble to understand China's traditions and show that their concern for China grew not out contempt for its civilization, but out of a profound and informed respect.

It's my privilege to be the current president of the PEN American Center, one of the 145 PEN International centers around the world, members of the literary community working together to support free expression and international cultural exchange. In our work in support of Liu Xiaobo, we are guided at every step by our colleagues in the Independent Chinese PEN Center, insiders who are working, as he has done, to serve the cause of freedom in their country. With their guidance, we are able to participate from outside China in shaping its development. We can do so in part because the Chinese, like all people, want to be respected in the community of nations. Yet such full-hearted respect is denied them when the regime denies the rights of its own people, and that forces government officials to deal with the fact that they are denying *themselves* the respect they need.

Yesterday, a Chinese exile told me that what she feels when she reads about the abuses of people like Liu is shame. We have to work with China's human rights community to lift that burden of shame, so that the Chinese can have the respect of all of us because they have done what it takes to deserve it. Honor and shame are powerful motivators. Honoring Liu Xiaobo supports him in his work. But the shame of what the government of China is doing to him is driving many of his fellow citizens to line up alongside him.

Democracy Has Failed in Many Developing Nations

N.S. Venkataraman

N.S. Venkataraman is an Indian journalist, blogger, and founder of the nongovernmental organization Nandini Voice for the Deprived.

Almost every developing country in the world except a few countries like Myanmar and North Korea claim that theirs is a democratic governance. Obviously, democracy as a concept is viewed as the most desirable form of governance and people of every country would like to jump into this bandwagon.

Bitter Animosity

However, in actual practice, in many developing countries in Asia, Africa and Latin America, the process of democracy is marked by bitter animosity and quarrel between the different political parties, giving an impression as if these countries are in constant turmoil all the time with one group trying to defeat another group to seize power. Large segments of the population of these countries who are not part of the political groups, remain as mere spectators in this so called democratic process and often feel frustrated and helpless. Such people who are not part of any political group many times wonder whether this sort of democracy has done any overall good to the country at all.

What the discerning common people note is that the difference between the political parties in these countries are not due to any fundamental difference in policies and programmes but only due to the personal ambition of the leaders of the political groups.

Of course, elections do take place in these developing countries at periodical intervals, where a ruling group can be dislodged in a smooth manner if desired by the people. But, the problem is that these elections are being contested by different political groups who are bitterly opposed to each other and they conduct themselves during the electioneering and thereafter as if they are in the midst of a warfare. They give an impression that they are sworn personal enemies exhibiting a sort of hatred towards each other and may go to any extent to destroy each other in their bid to capture power and enjoy the benefits of power thereafter.

> *In actual practice, in many developing countries in Asia, Africa and Latin America, the process of democracy is marked by bitter animosity . . . between the different political parties.*

Even More Deterioration

In recent times, there have been even more deterioration in the quality of democracy practiced in the developing countries, in that several political groups (political parties) are now controlled by families of the political leaders that would inevitably lead to family rule and a sort of feudalism. In the process, the political groups become outfits sans any ideology, with the party cadre pledging loyalty to one political family or the other.

With the family members getting a stranglehold on the political parties to achieve their ambitions of seizing power, philosophy, principles and ideology do not have any significant place any more. What becomes priority to the politicians is only the upliftment of their family members and achievement of their ambitions to seize power and for this they "skillfully" work out schemes to outdo others. In the process, a few political groups (political families) align between themselves to outdo another aligned force and this is what is now known as coalition politics.

Each political group in its anxiety to defeat the other often even goes to the extent of maintaining thugs and rowdies in their groups to indulge in violence, settle scores with the opponents, indulge in malpractices in elections, including bribing the voters etc. Due to this approach, the law and order machinery virtually collapses.

When personal ambitions of the political leaders and the needs of their families become the most important factors, the progress of the country inevitably suffers and the democracy becomes a counter productive movement. Several developing countries seem to be rapidly moving towards this condition.

In such a scenario, democracy loses its purpose and significance and people become disillusioned. The people may then probably think that the rule by a dictator and his family could be even less harmful than this sort of several political groups and their family members spread all over the country and ruling the nation.

When personal ambitions of the political leaders . . . become the most important factors, . . . democracy becomes a counter productive movement.

The Case of Sri Lanka

After the ethnic war, when Sri Lanka went for presidential elections, it caught worldwide attention and even admiration to some extent as a vibrant democracy. But all these became anticlimax when the political groups and presidential candidates fought the elections, bitterly abusing each other as if they are sworn enemies.

After the poll, the opponent presidential candidate was arrested and is now facing trial, confirming the suspicions of many that the political parties and their leaders have no bigger target than outdoing one another, unconcerned about the consequences to the national welfare and progress.

It appears that the process of democracy is only a tool for these politicians to climb to power and to control the government and the country and enjoy power and authority for their families and their followers.

On the other hand, the votaries of democracy expect that these political groups should contest the elections on the basis of policies and programmes and should really be competing with each other to provide greater service and benefits to the people and country at large.

In such a situation, democracy as a concept appears to have failed in many developing countries. This is certainly a very unfortunate condition since the developing countries have millions of citizens living below the poverty line and they desperatively need meaningful and progressive programmes of the government. Such expectations of the people will not be met by ambitious and self serving politicians who have emerged in the democratic system that are now being practiced in the developing countries.

Revolution in Egypt Could Lead to Instability and Anti-Americanism

Susan Estrich

Susan Estrich is an American lawyer, professor, author, and po-litical commentator. She was the campaign manager for Demo-crat Michael Dukakis's 1988 presidential run.

In the first days of the [2011] demonstrations in Egypt, al-most everyone I know was glued to their television. Many of them were caught up in what they saw as the romanticism of the moment: students and young people in the streets, will-ing to risk their lives to stand up to a tyrannical regime and replace it with a democracy. Irresistible.

Television anchors jumped on planes to report from the middle of the demonstrations. Commentators waxed eloquent about the power of new technology and social media to bring freedom and democracy to countries long under the thumb of tyrannical rulers. What could be more exciting or, for that matter, more American?

As it turns out, a lot of things.

The anchors who went came back almost as fast—revolu-tions are dangerous. [CNN anchor] Anderson Cooper was not a hero among the masses. Maybe they didn't know who he was, although a guy surrounded by cameras and film equip-ment who appears on international television every day is not that hard to recognize. Maybe, more likely, they didn't care.

This is not the American Revolution broadcasting from Cairo.

Economic Motivations

It is true, of course, that Egypt is not a democracy. It is true that Hosni Mubarak has held power for three decades. It is certainly true that during that period many Egyptians have called—without success—for greater freedom, free elections, free press and an open democracy. But most of those people are not on the streets.

"It's the economy, stupid," the smartest observers keep pointing out. People have been on the streets in Cairo and not Beijing [China's capital] because, first and foremost, Egypt's economy has grown much slower than its population, while China's is the exact opposite. The streets in Cairo are not necessarily filled with well-educated ideologues but with frustrated job-seekers, young people who have found not opportunity but closed doors in their home country.

This is not the American Revolution broadcasting from Cairo.

The rallying cry has been "Replace Mubarak." But the motivation is as much economic as it is political.

Rejecting the West

And equally if not more troubling, to the extent that it is political, it is not about emulating the West, but rejecting it. The voices from the street are not just saying that Mubarak has been in power too long, or even that he has failed to pursue policies leading to greater economic growth.

They are saying he has been too supportive of the West, too close to the United States and, even more importantly, too close to, too supportive of and too engaged with Israel.

They are saying that one of the best and most courageous things Mubarak has done—despite some difficult periods, he maintained relations with Israel and recognized its existence—is reason enough for his downfall.

I have a hard time finding anything romantic about that.

Many young people today don't remember the days of "realpolitik"—the idea, popular during the Cold War, that America's foreign policy should be based on our national interest and not on ideology, meaning we supported dictators who liked us without regard to how they treated their people. The downfall of the policy, depending on your politics, was either our victory in the Cold War (which might have proved that it worked) or the repeated downfall of the dictators we supported (which might have proved that it didn't). If you're giving a speech at a convention, it always sounds better to say that our foreign policy must be based on our values; that our goal should be to support freedom and democracy, even if that results in leaders we like less.

Revolution is . . . a rather terrifying thriller with no guarantee of a happy ending.

It sounds very good. But in a dangerous world, what sounds good is not always what will work well, what will protect our country and our allies and our children.

As Mubarak steps down, I am rooting for Egypt. I'm rooting for it to find a way out of these troubles, to restore the economic growth whose absence fuels such anger, to find a path to greater individual freedom and participatory democracy.

But I am also rooting for us, and for our friends in Israel, that Egypt's path will not bring greater instability and danger to our world. Revolution is not a romantic adventure. It's a rather terrifying thriller with no guarantee of a happy ending.

China Exemplifies Anti-Democratic Success in the Developing World

Joshua Kurlantzick and Perry Link

Joshua Kurlantzick is a fellow for Southeast Asia at the Council on Foreign Relations, an independent, nonpartisan membership organization, think tank, and publisher. He is also a special correspondent for the New Republic, *a columnist for* Time, *and a senior correspondent for the* American Prospect, *as well as the author of the book* Charm Offensive: How China's Soft Power Is Transforming the World. *Perry Link is professor emeritus of East Asian studies at Princeton University and Chancellorial Chair for Teaching Across Disciplines at the University of California–Riverside. He has published widely on modern Chinese language, literature, and popular thought.*

In a relatively short period of time, China has built close diplomatic and economic relations with a wide range of countries across the developing world. In fact, as a result of its charm offensive, China's public image in many developing states is currently far more positive than that of any other major power, even as its efforts in places like North America and Europe founder on human rights concerns and trade disputes. This charm offensive is partly an expression of Chinese "soft power." Many Chinese scholars and officials view soft power more broadly than [Harvard professor] Joseph Nye, the originator of the term. Whereas Nye described it as the attractive appeal of a country's values, the CCP [Chinese Communist Party] definition would encompass virtually any mechanism outside of the military and security sphere, including tools that Nye considered coercive, like aid and investment. President Hu Jintao and other party leaders have clearly embraced the idea of soft power, and it has become central to their discourse about China's role in the world. While only five years ago Chinese officials and academics vehemently denied that they had any lessons to offer to the developing world, today they not only accept this idea but use their training programs for foreign officials to promote aspects of the China model of development.

Authoritarian Soft Power

One of the tools China has used to expand its international influence and promote its model of governance is the fast-growing network of Confucius Institutes. The institutes, which provide instruction in Chinese language and culture, typically operate as partnerships between Chinese universities and a university in the host country, with the latter supplying a site and other facilities, and the former providing the staff and teaching materials. The centers are supervised by the Chinese Language Council International which sets their guiding principles, budget, and curriculum. The council is composed of representatives from 12 state ministries and commissions, including the ministries of education, foreign affairs, and culture. The Confucius Institutes initiative describes its purpose as "enhancing intercultural understanding in the world by sponsoring courses of Chinese language and culture, so as to promote a better understanding of the Chinese language and culture among the people of the world." However, some observers have raised concerns about the potential effects of Chinese state influence on academic freedom in the host countries. A set of draft guidelines for the institutes suggests that Chinese authorities would require them to comply with political directives on sensitive issues, such as Taiwan's international status or historical inquiry related to persecuted ethnic and religious minorities: "Overseas Confucius Institutes must abide by the One-China Policy, preserve the independence and unity of the People's Republic of China, and . . . refrain from participating in any political, religious or ethnic activities in the country where they are located." The network has expanded rapidly since the first institute opened in Uzbekistan in 2004. There are now more than 295 of the centers in 78 countries, with a total of 500 set to be established before 2010. The existing institutes include more than 20 in Southeast Asia, over 40 in the United States, and more than 70 in Europe. Others have been founded in African countries, including Zimbabwe and South Africa. The project has entailed the deployment of more than 2,000 staff members, and more than 300,000 sets of textbooks and audio materials worth over $26 million.

China's public image in many developing states is currently far more positive than that of any other major power.

In discussing soft power, CCP officials stress the training programs, effective traditional diplomacy, the growth of public diplomacy projects like the Confucius Institutes, and the appeal of China's economic example, which has sparked particular interest in Africa, Central Asia, and Southeast Asia. However, in the long run China's rulers will need to broaden their appeal to reach the general populations of developing countries. In addition, they may have to expand or adjust their soft power initiative to make headway in the developed world, particularly in Europe, where there may be more favorable sentiment than in the United States.

The Purpose of Soft Power

The CCP leadership's rationale for pursuing soft power is complex. For one thing, it has become more confident and sophisticated in global affairs. The current generation of officials apparently recognized that Beijing must actively cultivate its relations with developing Asian, African, and Latin American countries. China's growing economic, political, and security interdependence with the world, and its demand for natural resources, has forced it to play a larger role in international affairs, while a series of events that were detrimental to America's public image, from the Asian financial crisis to the Iraq war, provided opportunities for a rising power to chip away at the influence of the United States and its allies. In another sense, the wars in Afghanistan and Iraq showcased the overwhelming power and technology of the U.S. military, indicating to the CCP that its hard-power alternatives were limited.

Finally, as China's economic growth has continued without a strong democratic challenge from the new middle class, as other authoritarian states like Russia have also produced high growth rates, and as the economies of established democracies have suffered repeated shocks over the past five years, CCP officials have begun to consider the possibility that their model of development—rather than representing a tactical compromise between communism and free enterprise—might actually be a coherent and exportable system that is objectively superior to liberal democratic capitalism. To articulate and sell this idea, CCP leaders have increasingly appropriated the term "democracy" and applied it to their own arrangement. Much as the [Russian] Kremlin under Vladimir Putin described its authoritarian manipulations as "guided democracy," the CCP has twisted the word beyond recognition and stripped off the values that have traditionally defined it. In addition, Chinese officials, academics, and media increasingly point to unrest in places like Kenya and Kyrgyzstan to suggest that Western, liberal democracy is not appropriate for many developing countries.

China's Tools and Strategies

Over the past decade, China has centered its global outreach on one core philosophy. In statements and speeches, Chinese leaders enunciate a doctrine of win-win (shuangying) relations, encouraging Latin American, African, Asian, and Arab states to form mutually beneficial arrangements with China. Win-win relations also focus on the principle of noninterference, which is particularly relevant for developing-world leaders who witnessed decades of intervention by colonial powers and Cold War antagonists.

[Chinese] officials have begun to consider . . . that their model of development . . . might actually be a coherent and exportable system that is objectively superior to liberal democratic capitalism.

CCP leaders extend the win-win idea to a range of other arenas, claiming to stand on the side of developing countries in global trade talks and portraying China as a defender of noninterference at the United Nations. As part of this strategy, the win-win philosophy is implicitly contrasted with that of the West, which Beijing portrays as pushing a uniform "democracy agenda" onto developing nations. While upgrading its diplomatic corps and using high-level traditional diplomacy to show developing states that China places a high priority on bilateral relations, China's government has also begun founding its own regional multilateral organizations, like the Shanghai Cooperation Organization (SCO) in Central Asia, which it can use to counter the promotion of democracy. Many foreign leaders have been receptive to China's bid for international leadership. "You are an example of transformation," Madagascar president Marc Ravalomanana told Chinese officials during the May 2007 African Development Bank meeting in Shanghai. "We in Africa must learn from your success."

The CCP also seems to have recognized that it needs to build a broader public appeal and improve people-to-people contacts. This is a critical change from the past approach, which focused almost exclusively on forging relationships with foreign leaders. Beijing has developed the China Association of Youth Volunteers, a Peace Corps—like program designed to bring young people to countries like Ethiopia to work on agricultural and language projects. It has also launched the Confucius Institute project to support Chinese language and cultural studies at universities around the globe. It increasingly provides funding for Chinese language primary schools in developing countries like Cambodia; students who succeed in these schools often receive scholarships for university study in China.

> *Beijing portrays [the West] as pushing a uniform "democracy agenda" onto developing nations.*

Training programs for foreign opinion leaders have similarly become a significant soft power instrument. The Chinese government has begun organizing training programs for media workers and law enforcement officials from Central Asia, Africa, and Southeast Asia, among other regions. These programs are designed in part to showcase the success of China's economic strategy, which involves partial liberalization, protection of certain industries, and maintenance of some degree of state intervention.

Development assistance may be China's most important tool. China has proven especially willing to step up aid to countries like Uzbekistan and Cambodia after other donors express concerns over human rights. It has also dramatically boosted its investment in and trade with developing countries, with the investment often supported by loans on favorable terms. In speeches, CCP leaders suggest that Beijing will be a fairer trading partner than established democracies, helping poorer countries to obtain the technology and skills they need to develop and enrich themselves. With developed countries, too, China tries to emphasize its role as an influential trading partner in order to win other concessions; in the wake of the global financial crisis, China has emphasized that with its massive currency reserves, it will play a proactive role in managing and combating the downturn. However, these inroads are complicated by popular sentiment in industrialized countries that often blames China for domestic job losses.

China's Outreach Threatens Democracy

The CCP's soft-power tools mean different things to China's various international partners. It is important to differentiate between the types of government Beijing has relationships with, and to examine the ways in which these relationships imperil democracy. On the one hand, there is a group of harsh regimes—including those of Sudan, Burma, Uzbekistan, North Korea, and Zimbabwe—whose leaders are seeking only financial assistance and protection at the United Nations and other international bodies. Other tools of soft power are largely irrelevant for these governments, and they have little interest in learning about China's pursuit of economic reform. On the other hand, there is a diverse group of developing countries across Asia, Latin America, and Africa that are receptive to all elements of Chinese soft power. They are seeking economic, political, and cultural ties to China, and because they are not purely authoritarian states, China's allure can extend to the public. These relationships can be more substantial than a simple alliance with an autocrat or ruling clique.

When Beijing initially began building its soft-power strategy, it did not directly threaten global democratization to the same extent as, for example, Russia's strategy under Putin, which was designed from the beginning to push back against democratic reforms in neighboring countries. However, the "color revolutions" in the former Soviet Union frightened the CCP, while the rise of other authoritarian great powers emboldened Beijing to believe that it might have a transferable model. Furthermore, nationalism began to build up within

China, and the entire democracy promotion movement faced a global backlash. As a result, the CCP's strategies began to target democracy promotion more aggressively. Over the past decade China has revamped its visitor training programs to more stridently tout the China model and in many ways to belittle liberal democracy. Today, many of these programs focus almost exclusively on the study of a Chinese example of the topic covered, whether economic institution building, local governance, or the creation of a judicial system.

The training programs often involve discussions of how the CCP has managed to open its economy, keep the middle class on the side of the government, and avoid sociopolitical chaos like that experienced during the transition periods in Russia and many other developing economies. In particular, China has begun large-scale training programs for police, judges, and other security officials from neighboring nations. Since internet filtering and control has been a significant component of China's regime maintenance, training in these methods is also offered to some foreign officials. The Chinese government has provided information and strategies on filtering and firewalling to Burma, Vietnam, Saudi Arabia, Uzbekistan, and several other states.

The scale of this effort is difficult to calculate, but each year the Chinese government trains at least 1,000 Central Asian judicial and police officials, most of whom could be classified as working in antidemocratic enterprises. Over the long term, Beijing plans to step up its training programs for African officials to reach 7,000 to 10,000 trainees per year. The scope of China's broader aid programs is similarly impossible to quantify, but the World Bank estimates that China is now the largest lender to Africa. At a 2007 gathering in Shanghai, Chinese leaders announced that they would offer Africa $20 billion in new financing.

Chinese aid now outstrips that of democratic donor countries in a range of Southeast Asian and Central Asian states.

Cambodia, one of Beijing's major aid beneficiaries, provides an instructive example. The Chinese government is Cambodia's largest provider of military aid, most of which goes to anti-democratic security forces that are used as a political weapon by Prime Minister Hun Sen. China has pledged a total of some $600 million in assistance to Cambodia. By comparison, the United States currently provides Cambodia with roughly $55 million in annual aid. The case of Burma shows similar trends. China's government is now the largest provider of assistance, which again is used mainly for antidemocratic activities. Beijing has provided two $200 million loans to Burma over the past five years, and these "soft" loans are often never repaid, essentially making them grants. The United States provides roughly $12 million in annual aid to Burma, mostly for humanitarian and refugee assistance.

Chinese aid now outstrips that of democratic donor countries in a range of Southeast Asian and Central Asian states.

These training and aid relationships allow Beijing and its partner governments to provide mutual assistance with their respective domestic concerns. Security training for Central Asian officials, for example, has provided an opportunity for the CCP to promote the idea that Uyghurs [a Muslim separatist group in China] are terrorists and separatists, and that they threaten regional stability. This process has paid off over the past decade, as several Central Asian states have begun repatriating Chinese Uyghurs, often with no cause. Like Russia, Beijing is also beginning to develop its own NGOs [nongovernmental organizations], some of which are designed to mimic traditional democracy-promotion groups. Rather than building democratic institutions, however, they advise Southeast and Central Asian countries on political and economic development as part of an effort to push back against democratization.

Perhaps the most dangerous aspect of China's growing global presence is that its government now is able to offer more extensive diplomatic protection and support to the authoritarian rulers of countries like Burma, Sudan, Uzbekistan, and Zimbabwe. The SCO [Shanghai Cooperation Organization], created by Beijing as a counterweight to U.S. and European influence in Central Asia, plays a pivotal role in this strategy. Both China and Russia have utilized SCO forums to criticize the promotion of democracy and to support Central Asian autocrats as they suppress domestic calls for reform and democratic change.

If Beijing proves flexible enough to use its soft power on . . . the developing world, it could mount a serious challenge to . . . democracy.

Challenges for Beijing

At the United Nations, Beijing has checked international pressure on human rights abusers like Burma and exploited such moments to improve its bilateral relations with the regime concerned. Soon after the Andijon massacre in 2005 led to increased U.S. and European sanctions on Uzbekistan, China hosted the Uzbek leadership in Beijing and used the opportunity to increase its access to Uzbek natural resources. This pattern is not seen in every case, of course; China has actively cooperated with the international community in managing a recalcitrant North Korea. But this is largely because Beijing sees instability in North Korea as a direct threat to China, and its agenda for that country certainly does not include human rights promotion.

It remains unclear whether China's soft-power offensive will succeed in the long run. Many developing states worry that the character of trade links with Beijing, which often focus on the extraction of their natural resources, will prevent them from climbing the value-added ladder. This sentiment finds voice in populist politicians like Zambia's Michael Sata, who used anti-China sentiment to rally support in the 2006 presidential election, though his bid for office was ultimately unsuccessful. The fact that large, state-linked Chinese energy and construction companies habitually use transplanted Chinese workers for overseas projects does not endear them to local populations.

Furthermore, as Beijing grows more aggressive in its promotion of the antidemocratic China model, it risks becoming the mirror image of the Western powers it criticizes; it will be "intervening" in other countries' internal affairs, but to squelch rather than to promote democracy. Although Beijing's vows of noninterference appear to be welcomed, some leaders in the developing world are already wondering whether China is committed to this principle. The Chinese ambassador to Zambia in 2006 warned that Beijing might cut off diplomatic ties if voters chose Sata as their president. As the honeymoon period with Beijing comes to an end, civil society groups in countries that receive Chinese aid will begin to speak out more. Many activists are coming to realize that Chinese assistance can contribute to environmental destruction, poor labor standards, rampant graft, and backsliding on democratic consolidation. Still, if Beijing proves flexible enough to use its soft power on both leaders and the public in the developing world, it could mount a serious challenge to the established values, ideas, and models of democracy.

CHAPTER 4

What Can Be Done to Aid the Developing World?

Chapter Preface

In just the last few decades, information technology (IT) has permeated society and transformed life for people and businesses in industrialized countries. In the United States, for example, more than 90 percent of Americans have cellphones, and around 70 percent have access to the Internet. Similar levels of access exist in other Western nations such as Canada and the countries in Europe. In this developed world, technology has changed almost every aspect of modern living, including how companies do business, how research and education is conducted, how politicians raise money for their campaigns, and how people communicate and socialize with each other. Many developing nations, however, still have very limited or virtually no access to digital and information technology. This gap in technology access between the developed and the developing world is often referred to as the digital divide. Yet today there is widespread interest—not only in poor countries themselves but also at the United Nations and among the makers of technology products—in spreading technology more widely. Many experts predict that coming years will offer an explosion of technology in poorer, less-developed nations.

When many people think of technology, they often think of the personal computer and the Internet because those are the technologies that have spearheaded the technological revolution in the United States and other developed countries. But technology also includes a wide range of other IT devices, as well as tools with applications in industry, government, education, research, and almost every other sector. In developing countries, for example, the most popular technology is the cellphone. According to technology experts, billions of people now own cellphones around the world. The rapid spread of wireless technology and the relatively low cost of cellphones have meant that telephone reception is available almost everywhere, even in some of the most remote parts of the world.

In fact, the cellphone is quickly becoming a must-have technology in many developing countries. Cellphones give people the power to access information, not only social information, but also information critical to running businesses and earning a living. With just a phone call, for example, farmers can compare prices being offered for produce and harvests in order to sell at the highest price; fishermen can check markets for fish even before returning to the dock; and a variety of individuals and small businesses can communicate with customers to sell their goods and services or otherwise line up future work. In some remote communities, the purchase of a cellphone has even resulted in the creation of a new business model—one in which the cellphone owner charges people in the village who do not have phones to make individual calls.

The spread of cellphones in poorer countries illustrates that the path technology will take in poorer, so-called Third World regions may be quite different from how technology was developed and is used in wealthier nations. Experts explain that developing nations may leapfrog over certain technologies, such as computers, and be more interested in cheaper items such as cellphones. The development and spread of cellphones that can easily access the Internet through wireless technology is expected to bring even more information and power into the hands of people in the developing world. Some foreign policy experts think technology may become a strong force for global economic development as well as a tool to attack global poverty.

As the technology wave reaches developing countries, it also could have significant influence on politics and governments, especially autocratic regimes that have historically repressed citizens and restricted their access to information. Already, the world has seen citizen uprisings in which cellphones and Internet technologies have been critical not only in revealing information about corruption and repression by government but also in coordinating and organizing protests and demonstrations against ruling regimes. Recent examples include Tunisia and Egypt, where protest marches were staged and broadcast around the world via cellphones and Internet social media sites. In both nations, protesters succeeded in overturning the ruling government and forcing the country's president out of office.

Technology manufacturers—both hardware and software companies—are anxious to tap what could be a huge worldwide market for their goods and services. Many companies are developing products especially tailored to appeal to emerging economies. For example, Motorola has developed a simple and inexpensive cellphone, the Motofone, specifically for developing countries. It provides up to 400 hours of usage on one battery charge, and has a large screen that works without internal lighting that could use up battery power—useful for places where electrical plug-ins are scarce. Similarly, the Massachusetts Institute of Technology (MIT) has developed a $100 laptop computer designed for schoolchildren in developing regions that can also be read as a book. In fact, some of the most well-known technology companies are also focusing on serving this new, potentially enormous market, including Microsoft, Google, Intel, and Nokia. The good news is that as companies begin addressing larger and larger markets, the cost of electronic devices will surely go down while products continue to grow in complexity. Many interested observers hope that this will help to provide people in developing nations highly sophisticated yet inexpensive technologies that will rival those in the developed world. If these types of products can be created, manufacturers will likely find a long line of eager people hungry to purchase them.

Spreading technological access is one of the most exciting ways that individuals, companies, and industrialized nations can help to uplift developing nations. The authors of the viewpoints in this chapter discuss a variety of other ideas to aid the developing world.

Foreign Aid Is Needed to Eradicate Hunger and Prevent Failed States

Joshua Kurlantzick

Joshua Kurlantzick is a fellow for Southeast Asia at the Council on Foreign Relations, an independent, nonpartisan membership organization, think tank, and publisher. He is also a special correspondent for the New Republic, *a columnist for* Time, *and a senior correspondent for the* American Prospect, *as well as the author of the 2007 book* Charm Offensive: How China's Soft Power Is Transforming the World.

A t the last G8 [a group of the world's eight wealthiest nations] summit in June [2010] the world's leading nations agreed to work hard on the usual litany of good causes—peace, global warming, etc.—with one notable exception. The issue that had dominated the summit just five years ago, foreign aid, got little mention. Perhaps that's not surprising, given how many rich nations are busy bailing themselves out of the debt crisis, but it is emblematic of a wider malaise: the death of generosity itself.

Reversals on Aid

Just a decade ago, most Western economies were still thriving, and sitting Western leaders like [British prime minister] Tony Blair and [US president] Bill Clinton were signing on to high-profile celebrity campaigns to boost public and private aid to the developing world. [Singer/musician of band U2] Bono became a global celebrity all over again, as a development expert. The Live 8 concerts and Global Call to Action Against Poverty Day of 2005 brought together tens of millions of concerned citizens from around the world; economist Jeffrey Sachs's book on ending poverty through a massive new infusion of aid became a bestseller. In the [George W.] Bush White House, the (empirically dubious) idea that poverty breeds terrorism gave rise to the Millennium Challenge Corporation, designed to boost aid and reward well-governed recipient nations. This attention paid off. Between 2001 and 2005, governments around the world more than doubled their allocations of foreign aid, setting the stage for the optimism of the 2005 G8 summit in Gleneagles, Scotland, at which all the G8 nations except Russia vowed to pitch in to a new $50 billion aid package to the world's poorest countries, including $25 billion annually to Africa. This new flow of aid was designed to help the poorest countries achieve the United Nations Millennium Development Goals for 2015, which included eradicating extreme poverty and hunger, and achieving universal primary education.

In April [2010] . . . foreign aid from wealthy nations had actually fallen by $3.5 billion between 2008 and 2009 and was not going to meet its previous targets.

Private donors also opened their wallets. In 2006 [Microsoft founder and billionaire philanthropist] Bill Gates persuaded fellow billionaire Warren Buffett to bequeath most of his fortune to the Gates Foundation, nearly doubling its assets and creating a philanthropy with more power than any the world has ever seen, devoted primarily to putting an end to deadly Third World diseases.

Yet by 2010, the Organization for Economic Cooperation and Development found that the G8 was on track to break its 2005 commitment, and would likely provide Africa with less than half the money pledged. Other studies suggested worse news. In April the NGO [nongovernmental organization] Oxfam observed that foreign aid from wealthy nations had actually fallen by $3.5 billion between 2008 and 2009 and was not going to meet its previous targets. Italy's aid spending dropped by 31 percent; Germany's by 12 percent; Japan's by 11 percent; and Canada's by 9.5 percent. In June the G8 nations acknowledged that they had donated only $6.5 billion of the $20 billion promised for the L'Aquila Food Security Initiative, designed to fight hunger and poverty in developing nations. The world now seems unlikely to meet the Millennium Development Goals by 2015.

Even in Afghanistan, the poor nation now most important to U.S. foreign policy, aid numbers have not matched promises. In 2002 President George W. Bush pledged the equivalent of a Marshall Plan for Afghanistan, but according to Peter Bergen, an expert on Afghanistan at the New America Foundation, he never delivered. Bush raised humanitarian assistance to Afghanistan from $1.3 billion in 2004 to $1.9 billion in 2008, but that's still a sum far lower than what Washington gave to rebuild the Balkans in the 1990s, and it represents a much lower share of U.S. GDP [gross domestic product, a measure of a country's economic output] than the Marshall Plan commitment to rebuild postwar Europe.

One big obstacle to aid is the politics of spending money on other nations' problems. President Bush enjoyed a [Richard] Nixon-goes-to-China credibility with conservatives, who tend to be more skeptical of foreign aid. But [President Barack] Obama's low popularity among conservative voters makes it nearly impossible for him to sell an aid program to them. Reaching out in this way might feed into American stereotypes that Republicans are tougher on national security while Democrats prefer soft power.

What's more, Americans are not in a generous mood. In a poll released last December [2009] by the Pew research organization, nearly half the Americans surveyed said that the U.S. should "mind its own business" in the world. This figure was the highest level of support for isolationism in decades. And it is not just the U.S.; polls show that this isolationism is matched in many wealthy nations in Europe and Asia, including Japan, long one of the biggest donor nations.

It is not surprising that nations such as Italy, one of the weakest industrialized economies, have slashed their aid budgets by more than 30 percent, while France has not met promised commitments, and the Obama administration has presided over reductions in the budget of the Millennium Challenge Corporation from $3 billion requested for 2008 to $1.4 billion this year.

Even in Afghanistan, the poor nation now most important to U.S. foreign policy, aid numbers have not matched promises.

Corruption in Developing Nations

Recipient nations have not exactly helped themselves. In the early 2000s many developing countries eagerly pledged to improve governance in order to make aid more effective. In 2001 African nations agreed to a New Partnership for Africa's Development, a continent-wide compact to improve governance, promote equitable development, fight graft, and fulfill other aims favored by both Western donors and civil-society activists in most developing nations. In 2006 wealthy Sudanese communications entrepreneur Mo Ibrahim established a $5 million prize for the African leader who best focused on development, governance, and education. Yet the performance of these aid-recipient nations often has been woefully poor, a failure that only further alienates donors. Kenya, for one, vowed in 2002 to implement a tougher reform program, appointing prominent graft fighter John Githongo as anti-corruption czar. Within two years, Githongo had been forced out of real power, and he soon fled the country, his investigations having failed to change Kenya's climate of corruption.

Githongo has since returned to Kenya to launch a grassroots advocacy group, but little has changed, though there is some hope that the new Constitution, passed in Kenya this month [August 2010], might curb some of the worst abuses. Still, Kenyan M.P.s [members of Parliament] recently voted themselves another salary increase, and now earn roughly $170,000 per year, nearly the same as members of the U.S. House of Representatives, though the average nominal annual income in Kenya is only about $900, compared with roughly $46,000 in the United States.

If the world fails to eradicate hunger ... children in many developing countries will still lack food, launching a cycle of stunted growth, weak brain development, and poor economic performance.

Unrealistic Expectations of Donors

In rich nations, the growing demand for instant political gratification also undermines the long-term commitment to aid programs. For instance, India, fueled partly by foreign assistance, launched the agricultural-modernization program that would come to be known as the green revolution in the early 1960s, but most of the results were not seen until the 1970s and even later. After the devastating Haiti earthquake last January [2010], governments and private citizens around the world rushed to contribute to the reconstruction effort, often pledging money through new tools such as mobile phones. But as the Haitian government, weak in the best of times, struggled to rebuild and resettle the homeless, many donors grew frustrated. Though it has been only seven months since the quake, only $506 million of the $5.3 billion pledged to the country has been disbursed. "Donors typically set unrealistic time frames for reconstruction, and the level of infrastructural and political damage inflicted in Haiti suggests that they must think in terms of years, if not decades," notes a report by Oxfam Great Britain on the Haitian disaster.

Private donors have struggled with the same challenges, especially because wealthy individuals are used to getting fast results in the business world and often cannot reproduce such quick successes through foreign philanthropy. In June [2010], Gates and Buffett launched a new campaign, named the Giving Pledge, to persuade other American billionaires to donate half their assets to charity, and roughly 40, including Los Angeles philanthropist Eli Broad, signed on. But that good news obscures the fact that there are hundreds of other billionaires who have decided to keep their wealth for themselves.

The Consequences of Cutting Aid

Slashing foreign aid might seem like a necessary evil when countries such as Italy or Britain could need bailing out. But reversing the G8 pledges will have severe consequences. For one thing, it means creating a gap for a new group of donors such as China and Venezuela to boost their aid commitments. These countries do not require the same sort of respect for human rights and high-quality governance that the West demands as a condition for aid. What's more, if the world fails to eradicate hunger, as vowed in the millennium goals, children in many developing countries will still lack food, launching a cycle of stunted growth, weak brain development, and poor economic performance; if the world does not meet the goal of universal primary education, African states may never catch up to East Asian competitors with strong primary-education systems.

In Afghanistan, and in many other countries, failed development can create failed states, which can breed radicalism and militancy. In *Foreign Policy* magazine's annual Failed States Index, the three "winners," Somalia, Chad, and Sudan, all happen to be humanitarian disaster zones. They are also places where instability has allowed powerful militant organizations to establish themselves and eventually threaten local institutions and Western ones. That could necessitate the use of more hard power by G8 nations, which is many times more expensive, in dollars and lives, than a proper investment in foreign aid.

Foreign Aid Will Not Help Developing Nations That Have Corrupt Governments

Rory Leishman

Rory Leishman is an author and columnist based in London, Ontario, Canada.

Over the past 30 years, Angola has developed into one of the world's major oil producers, yet it still ranks among the world's most impoverished countries. What has gone wrong?

Paul Collier has addressed this issue in *Plundered Planet: Why We Must—and How We Can—Manage Nature for Global Prosperity*. As Professor of Economics and Director of the Centre for the Study of African Economies at Oxford University, he is widely regarded as one of the leading authorities on the intractable economic problems besetting the world's least developed countries.

Corruption in Angola

In Angola, most oil production is managed by four major players—ExxonMobil, Shell, BP and Total. Some critics might suppose that these conglomerates have somehow contrived to siphon off most of the country's oil-export revenues, while leaving little for the government and the people of Angola, but that is simply not the case.

Foreign multinationals could easily plunder the natural resources of less developed countries during the colonial era. Today, these same companies and their successors are usually confronted by independent governments with ready access to an array of international banks and law firms that are eager to help auction off natural resources on the most favourable terms.

In this respect, Angola is typical. In the 1970s, the Angolan government established a national oil-company monopoly, Sonangol, with a mandate to manage the country's oil resources and acquire a 51 per cent interest in the subsidiaries of every foreign oil company operating in Angola. Since then, Sonangol has garnered huge revenues. Collier notes that in 2008, Angola took in more than twice as much in oil revenues than all the foreign aid disbursed to the world's least developed countries.

Clearly, some people in Angola are getting hugely rich from oil revenues while the majority of the population subsists in dire poverty. And the main reason for this tragedy is also evident: crooked government.

Nonetheless, the United Nations Human Development Report for 2009 lists Angola at 143rd in the world, just three levels higher than Bangladesh.

Correspondingly, the Institute for Democracy in Africa reports that while Angola has a GDP [gross domestic product, a measure of a country's economic output] per capita of about $4,400(US), "some 70 per cent of the population lives on less than a dollar a day."

Clearly, some people in Angola are getting hugely rich from oil revenues while the majority of the population subsists in dire poverty. And the main reason for this tragedy is also evident: crooked government.

Most of the billions of dollars paid to Sonangol by Exxon-Mobil, BP and other foreign companies for the right to produce and export oil from Angola has ended up in the bank accounts of the country's dictatorial President Jose Eduardo dos Santos and his military and government cronies.

The oppressed people of Angola have no choice but to put up with this transparent plundering of the nation's oil wealth by the country's own corrupt politicians and bureaucrats. Dos Santos will not brook any effective opposition. He assures that elections are fixed, the media are censored and public protests are severely curtailed.

A few years ago, some intrepid members of Angola's generally tame Parliament used to denounce government corruption. But even most of this parliamentary opposition to the regime fell silent after dos Santos started paying members $10(US) for every favourable vote.

Corruption Everywhere

Angola is not uniquely bad. Most other least developed countries are also ridden with corruption. To combat this evil, former British prime minister Tony Blair began the Extractive Industries Transparency Initiative, an international organization that promotes the voluntary disclosure of the payment, receipt and management of revenues from the oil, gas and mining industries.

> *No amount of foreign aid or natural-resource revenues can eradicate poverty ... in countries where corrupt rulers enrich themselves at the expense of their deeply impoverished fellow citizens.*

While most of the major multinationals in the West have agreed to go along with this initiative, Chinese companies have not. And neither has the government of Angola. In 2004, China's Eximbank extended a $2 billion loan to Angola for the ostensible purpose of rebuilding the country's infrastructure, but so far, most of this money has disappeared without a trace.

The sad conclusion is inescapable: Judging from experience in Angola and elsewhere, no amount of foreign aid or natural-resource revenues can eradicate poverty among the hundreds of millions of people trapped in countries where corrupt rulers enrich themselves at the expense of their deeply impoverished fellow citizens.

Developed Nations Must Reverse Their Development Policies to Reduce World Poverty

Walden Bello

Walden Bello is a senior analyst at Focus on the Global South, a program of Thailand's Chulalongkorn University's Social Research Institute, and a columnist for Foreign Policy in Focus, *a publication of the Institute for Policy Studies, a progressive think tank based in Washington, D.C.*

The issue of corruption resonates in developing countries. In the Philippines, for instance, the slogan of the coalition that is likely to win the 2010 presidential elections is "Without corrupt officials, there are no poor people."

Not surprisingly, the international financial institutions have weighed in. The World Bank has made "good governance" a major thrust of its work, asserting that the "World Bank Group focus on governance and anticorruption (GAC) follows from its mandate to reduce poverty—a capable and accountable state creates opportunities for poor people, provides better services, and improves development outcomes."

Corruption and Economic Growth

Because it erodes trust in government, corruption must certainly be condemned and corrupt officials resolutely prosecuted. Corruption also weakens the moral bonds of civil society on which democratic practices and processes rest. But although research suggests it has some bearing on the spread

Walden Bello, "Does Corruption Create Poverty?" *Foreign Policy in Focus*, April 21, 2010. www.fpif.org. Copyright © 2010. Reproduced by permission.

of poverty, corruption is not the *principal* cause of poverty and economic stagnation, popular opinion notwithstanding.

World Bank and Transparency International data show that the Philippines and China exhibit the same level of corruption, yet China grew by 10.3 percent per year between 1990 and 2000, while the Philippines grew by only 3.3 percent. Moreover, as a recent study by [teaching assistant] Shaomin Lee and [history professor] Judy Wu shows, "China is not alone; there are other countries that have relatively high corruption and high growth rates."

Limits of a Hegemonic Narrative

The "corruption-causes-poverty narrative" has become so hegemonic that it has often marginalized policy issues from political discourse. This narrative appeals to the elite and middle class, which dominate the shaping of public opinion. It's also a safe language of political competition among politicians. Political leaders can deploy accusations of corruption against one another for electoral effect without resorting to the destabilizing discourse of class.

The corruption-causes-poverty discourse is no doubt popular ... because it serves as a smokescreen for ... wrong policy choices of the more transparent technocrats.

Yet this narrative of corruption has increasingly less appeal for the poorer classes. Despite the corruption that marked his reign, [former Philippine president] Joseph Estrada is running a respectable third in the presidential contest in the Philippines, with solid support among many urban poor communities. But it is perhaps in Thailand where lower classes have most decisively rejected the corruption discourse, which the elites and Bangkok-based middle class deployed to oust Thaksin Shinawatra from the premiership in 2006.

While in power, Thaksin brazenly used his office to enlarge his corporate empire. But the rural masses and urban lower classes—the base of the so-called "Red Shirts"—have ignored this corruption and are fighting to restore his coalition to power. They remember the Thaksin period from 2001 to 2006 as a golden time. Thailand recovered from the Asian financial crisis after Thaksin kicked out the International Monetary Fund (IMF), and the Thai leader promoted expansionary policies with a redistributive dimension, such as cheap universal health care, a one-million-baht development fund for each town, and a moratorium on farmers' servicing of their debt. These policies made a difference in their lives.

Thaksin's Red Shirts are probably right in their implicit assessment that pro-people policies are more decisive than corruption when it comes to addressing poverty. Indeed, in Thailand and elsewhere, clean-cut technocrats have probably been responsible for greater poverty than the most corrupt politicians. The corruption-causes-poverty discourse is no doubt popular with elites and international financial institutions because it serves as a smokescreen for the structural causes of poverty, and stagnation and wrong policy choices of the more transparent technocrats.

The Philippines Case

The case of the Philippines since 1986 illustrates the greater explanatory power of the "wrong-policy narrative" than the corruption narrative. According to a historical narrative, massive corruption suffocated the promise of the post-[Ferdinand] Marcos democratic republic. In contrast, the wrong-policy narrative locates the key causes of Philippine underdevelopment and poverty in historical events and developments.

The complex of policies that pushed the Philippines into the economic quagmire over the last 30 years can be summed up by a formidable term: structural adjustment. Also known as neoliberal restructuring, it involves prioritizing debt repayment, conservative macroeconomic management, huge cutbacks in government spending, trade and financial liberalization, privatization and deregulation, and export-oriented production. Structural adjustment came to the Philippines courtesy of the World Bank, the IMF, and the World Trade Organization (WTO), but local technocrats and economists internalized and disseminated the doctrine.

Corazon Aquino [Phillipine president from 1986 to 1992] was personally honest—indeed the epitome of non-corruption—and her contribution to the reestablishment of democracy was indispensable. But her acceptance of the IMF's demand to prioritize debt repayment over development brought about a decade of stagnation and continuing poverty. Interest payments as a percentage of total government expenditures went from 7 percent in 1980 to 28 percent in 1994. Capital expenditures, on the other hand, plunged from 26 percent to 16 percent. Since government is the biggest investor in the Philippines—indeed in any economy—the radical stripping away of capital expenditures helps explain the stagnant 1 percent average yearly growth in gross domestic product in the 1980s, and the 2.3 percent rate in the first half of the 1990s.

In contrast, the Philippines' Southeast Asian neighbors ignored the IMF's prescriptions. They limited debt servicing while ramping up government capital expenditures in support of growth. Not surprisingly, they grew by 6 to 10 percent from 1985 to 1995, attracting massive Japanese investment, while the Philippines barely grew and gained the reputation of a depressed market that repelled investors.

When Aquino's successor, Fidel Ramos, came to power in 1992, the main agenda of his technocrats was to bring down all tariffs to 0–5 percent and bring the Philippines into the WTO and the ASEAN [Association of Southeast Asian Nations] Free Trade Area (AFTA), moves intended to make trade liberalization irreversible. A pick-up in the growth rate in the early years of Ramos sparked hope, but the green shoots were short-lived. Another neoliberal policy, financial liberalization, crushed this early promise. The elimination of foreign exchange controls and speculative investment restrictions attracted billions of dollars from 1993–1997. But this also meant that when panic hit Asian foreign investors in summer 1997, the same lack of capital controls facilitated the stampede of billions of dollars from the country in a few short weeks. This capital flight pushed the economy into recession and stagnation in the next few years.

The administration of the next president, Joseph Estrada, did not reverse course, and under the presidency of Gloria Macapagal Arroyo, neoliberal policies continued to reign. Over the next few years, the Philippine government instituted new liberalization measures on the trade front, entering into free-trade agreements with Japan and China despite clear evidence that trade liberalization was destroying the two pillars of the economy: industry and agriculture. Radical unilateral trade liberalization severely destabilized the Philippine manufacturing sector. The number of textile and garments firms, for instance, drastically reduced from 200 in 1970 to 10 in recent years. As one of Arroyo's finance secretaries admitted, "There's an uneven implementation of trade liberalization, which was to our disadvantage." While he speculated that consumers might have benefited from the tariff liberalization, he acknowledged that "it has killed so many local industries."

Taking advantage of the Third World debt crisis, the IMF and the World Bank imposed structural adjustment in over 70 developing countries in the course of the 1980s.

As for agriculture, the liberalization of the country's agricultural trade after the country joined the WTO in 1995 transformed the Philippines from a net food-exporting country into a net food-importing country after the mid-1990s. This year [2010] the China ASEAN Trade Agreement (CAFTA), negotiated by the Arroyo administration, goes into effect, and the prospect of cheap Chinese produce flooding the Philippines has made Filipino vegetable farmers fatalistic about their survival.

During the long Arroyo reign, the debt-repayment-oriented macroeconomic management policy that came with structural adjustment stifled the economy. With 20–25 percent of the national budget reserved for debt service payments because of the draconian Automatic Appropriations Law, government finances were in a state of permanent and widening deficit, which the administration tried to solve by contracting more loans. Indeed, the Arroyo administration contracted more loans than the previous three administrations combined.

Because of . . . trade liberalization, gains in economic growth and poverty reduction posted by developing countries in the 1960s and 1970s had disappeared by the 1980s and 1990s.

When the deficit reached gargantuan proportions, the government refused to declare a debt moratorium or at least renegotiate debt repayment terms to make them less punitive. At the same time, the administration did not have the political will to force the rich to take the brunt of bridging the deficit, by increasing taxes on their income and improving revenue collection. Under pressure from the IMF, the government levied this burden on the poor and the middle class by adopting an expanded value added tax (EVAT) of 12 percent on purchases. Commercial establishments passed on this tax to poor and middle-class consumers, forcing them to cut back on consumption. This then boomeranged back on small merchants and entrepreneurs in the form of reduced profits, forcing many out of business.

The straitjacket of conservative macroeconomic management, trade and financial liberalization, as well as a subservient debt policy, kept the economy from expanding significantly. As a result, the percentage of the population living in poverty increased from 30 to 33 percent between 2003 and 2006, according to World Bank figures. By 2006, there were more poor people in the Philippines than at any other time in the country's history.

Policy and Poverty in the Third World

The Philippine story is paradigmatic. Many countries in Latin America, Africa, and Asia saw the same story unfold. Taking advantage of the Third World debt crisis, the IMF and the World Bank imposed structural adjustment in over 70 developing countries in the course of the 1980s. Trade liberalization followed adjustment in the 1990s as the WTO, and later rich countries, dragooned developing countries into free-trade agreements.

> *Unless and until we reverse the policies of structural adjustment, trade liberalization, and conservative macroeconomic management, [developing nations] will not escape the poverty trap.*

Because of this trade liberalization, gains in economic growth and poverty reduction posted by developing countries in the 1960s and 1970s had disappeared by the 1980s and 1990s. In practically all structurally adjusted countries, trade liberalization wiped out huge swathes of industry, and countries enjoying a surplus in agricultural trade became deficit countries. By the beginning of the millennium, the number of people living in extreme poverty had increased globally by 28 million from the decade before. The number of poor increased in Latin America and the Caribbean, Central and Eastern Europe, the Arab states, and sub-Saharan Africa. The reduction in the number of the world's poor mainly occurred in China and countries in East Asia, which spurned structural readjustment policies and trade liberalization multilateral institutions and local neoliberal technocrats imposed on other developing economies.

China and the rapidly growing newly industrializing countries of East and Southeast Asia, where most of the global reduction in poverty took place, were marked by high degrees of corruption. The decisive difference between their performance and that of countries subjected to structural adjustment was not corruption but economic policy.

Despite its malign effect on democracy and civil society, corruption is not the main cause of poverty. The "anti poverty, anti-corruption" crusades that so enamor the middle classes and the World Bank will not meet the challenge of poverty. Bad economic policies create and entrench poverty. Unless and until we reverse the policies of structural adjustment, trade liberalization, and conservative macroeconomic management, we will not escape the poverty trap.

Population Control Policies in Developing Nations Must Focus on Helping Young Girls

Judith Bruce and John Bongaarts

Judith Bruce is a senior associate and policy analyst with the Poverty, Gender, and Youth Program of the Population Council, a nongovernmental organization that seeks to improve the reproductive health of people in developing nations. John Bongaarts is a Population Council vice president and distinguished scholar.

The demographic landscape has changed dramatically in the last forty years; now it is time for population policy to change in response. Early population programs focused on the "low-hanging fruit" of contraceptive supply—a strategy that made sense when few women in the developing world had access to family planning services. Today, we must reach into the higher branches. The population policy options outlined below address the two crucial levers of rapid population growth—high fertility and young age structure—with an array of supply and demand approaches. Moreover, these policies are vitally important to advance public health, gender equity, and social justice.

Investing in Girls

Investing in girls has always been a good idea—it is now even better in light of the shifting composition of future population growth. Investments in girls through adolescence provide a demographic "three-for": reducing population momentum by delaying marriage and childbearing, thereby increasing the space between generations; lowering desired family size as

Judith Bruce and John Bongaarts, "The New Population Challenge," *A Pivotal Moment: Population, Justice, and the Environmental Challenge*, Washington, DC: Island Press, 2009. Copyright © 2009 by Island Press. Reproduced by permission.

more educationally accomplished girls are less reliant on multiple children for security; and decreasing the age and power differential between partners, thus positively affecting women's ability to meet their fertility goals. Benefits also extend to the next generation, because those who marry later and with more authority are likely to invest in their children (especially their girl children) in ways that establish a virtuous cycle of improved health and education. Specifically, we must (1) help girls stay in school through adolescence, (2) provide social and economic alternatives to early marriage and childbearing, (3) end child marriage and support married girls, and (4) focus on the youngest first-time mothers.

Investing in girls has always been a good idea—it is now even better in light of the shifting composition of future population growth.

Help Girls Stay in School Through Adolescence. Girls' education has long been associated with positive developments in health and population outcomes. Attending school during adolescence is crucial to girls' reproductive health. Girls who stay in school during adolescence have later sexual initiation and are less likely to be sexually active than their same-age peers who are out of school. Those who are sexually active as students are also more likely to use contraceptives than their peers.

In recent decades, governments of developing countries have emphasized primary school attendance. Great progress has been made: Primary school attendance rates are up, and the gap between boys and girls is narrowing. Thus the new challenge is not just getting girls (and boys) to school on time but keeping them there through adolescence—minimizing dropout, especially around the time of puberty for girls. It is also important to increase the proportion of girls in the appropriate grade for their age: In most countries of sub-Saharan Africa, for example, the majority of adolescent girls in school are in primary grades.

Provide Social and Economic Alternatives to Early Marriage and Childbearing. In poor communities, early marriage, followed by early childbearing, is a vital security and survival strategy for girls. Girls (and their parents) may view marriage as the only possible economic choice and accepted social role. For young married girls, the failure to produce a child in a short period of time may make them vulnerable to unilateral divorce or abandonment. Thus, the opportunity costs of repeated childbearing outweigh any other possible choices they have.

Girls' education has long been associated with positive developments in health and population outcomes.

The vicious cycle of intergenerational poverty, high fertility, and poor health can be broken by concerted investments in the poorest girls in the poorest communities. In these communities, many voting people, especially girls, are permanently diverted in early adolescence from the path of school and access to decent work. The absence of sufficient investments in girls during the crucial ages around puberty—ages ten to fourteen—limits their prospects and encourages dependence on marital and sexual relationships and childbearing for social and economic security.

The promotion of girls' education to the secondary level and their inclusion in community development efforts, functional financial literacy, and publicly visible/civic activities offer girls the beginnings of autonomy and lays the foundations for shifting gender norms. Girls must have social power and economic authority to counter pressures for sexual relations as a livelihood strategy—both inside and outside of marriage.

End Child Marriage, Support Married Girls. Child marriage—legally, marriage of a girl or boy before her or his eighteenth birthday—is still with us. Demographic and health survey data indicate that in fifty less-developed countries, about 38 percent of young women aged twenty to twenty-four were married before age eighteen. If present patterns continue, over 100 million girls will be married as children in the next decade. Although the proportion of women who marry early is declining in most, but not all, parts of the world, it is vital to underscore that millions of girls are currently married, with many more in the pipeline. Child marriage is a practice that mainly affects girls (56 percent of women aged twenty to twenty-four versus 14 percent of men the same age were married by age twenty).

Marriage transforms virtually all aspects of girls' lives. Typically, a girl who marries is moved from her familiar home and village, loses contact with friends, is initiated into sexual activity with someone she barely knows, and soon becomes a mother. The implications for health and well-being are striking. Married girls have a higher risk for sexually transmitted infections and HIV than their sexually active unmarried peers. And the youngest (age sixteen and under) first-time mothers face an increased risk of mortality and morbidity—for themselves, and for their children.

Measures to eliminate child marriage must be context-specific and engage parents and community members. Essential elements of any strategy will be schooling in some form and giving girls better access to their peers. This can be achieved either through programs that promote primary to secondary school progression or that work with girls who have not been in school, creating group structures—assets in and of themselves and platforms through which the girls can receive functional literacy training, mentoring, health information, and either direct access to or referral to services.

At the same time, it is essential to invest in the 50-million-plus married girls in the developing world, whose social, economic, and reproductive lives are still ahead of them. We have had successful experiments with adolescent girls in a number of settings (Asia, Middle East, and Africa). "Married girls clubs" have been established to reduce social isolation, increase girls' agency and negotiating power with partners, and provide a venue for learning. These groups empower and connect married girls—a goal important in its own right and crucial to improving their health and well-being and that of their children.

Focus on the Youngest First-Time Mothers. Special measures need to be taken to make first-time pregnancy safer. First births carry special risks for both mother and child, regardless of the age of the mother. The issue is of particular relevance to married girls because the vast majority of births to adolescent girls are first births that occur within marriage. Adverse outcomes associated with first birth include obstructed labor (which can result in obstetric fistula in settings where access to care is limited), preeclampsia/eclampsia, malaria, and infant mortality. Disentangling the age and parity effects at young ages is difficult. But it is clear that the youngest first-time mothers—those under fifteen, owing to physical factors, and those under eighteen, owing to social factors—face special risks. Girls who give birth during adolescence require special attention because they are less mature and are simultaneously coping with their own and their baby's physiological, emotional, and economic needs.

Programs engaging the youngest first-time mothers are strategic from three perspectives. First, demographically, as fertility falls, a rising proportion of births will be first births. Second, habits formed around the first birth, such as infant feeding choices and, crucially, spacing through contraception, tend to be carried forward across the life cycle. Third, focusing the health system on the social needs of these first-time mothers will generally raise the quality of service-site interpersonal relations (caring about the context of the mother, developing support and communication with the father). These habits, embedded in the system, also tend to carry over to the ways in which women across all ages and parities are treated.

Improving Access to High-Quality, Appropriate Reproductive Health Services

When many family planning programs were launched in the 1960s and 1970s, there was a great unmet need for contraception, and most clients were married women. Clients and their needs have changed since those early years, and family planning programs must change with them, by providing a diverse array of services, including temporary contraception, and responding to social and emotional realities—including sexual coercion.

Providing a Diverse Array of Services, Including Temporary Contraception. Today, there is still a substantial unmet need for contraception and reproductive health care, in part because desired family size has declined substantially in a majority of developing countries. As women want fewer children, the number of years in which they must avoid pregnancy increases—and now approaches two decades, on average. But over the course of those decades, women and their partners will need a wider range of contraceptive and reproductive health services.

For example, a typical client is no longer a married woman seeking to end her childbearing years. More often, clinic waiting rooms are filled with young women or married couples who want to delay their first birth or ensure space between pregnancies. This means there is a need for technologies and services that allow couples to safely avoid childbearing without a loss of fertility. But some service providers still emphasize permanent methods of birth control, which are inappropriate for many young clients.

A key related trend is that more young women are being sexually initiated *outside* of marriage, long before they have established permanent partnerships. Young men and women need more and better information and services, and reversible methods—especially those that protect against sexually transmitted diseases, including HIV.

For decades, population policy has focused on the unmet need for contraceptive services. . . . But today's new population challenges require accelerated investment in human development.

Responding to Social and Emotional Realities—Including Sexual Coercion. Effective reproductive health services must also understand their clients' social and emotional needs. For example, sexual coercion is a serious problem, especially for young girls. In some settings, a very high proportion of first sexual relations may be tricked or forced. Thus, the social support and information at service points must build girls' agency and negotiating power. As the HIV epidemic becomes increasingly younger and female, service points and treatment alone are not sufficient to alter negative reproductive health outcomes that stem from HIV infection. This must be complemented by the expansion of single-sex safe and supportive spaces for girls. Such spaces can be established in youth clubs, community centers, religious institutions, and school facilities. Safe spaces are a primary asset to girls and young women, offering them access to peers and mentors and a base from which to offer or refer to services.

The Future for Population Policies

For decades, population policy has focused on the unmet need for contraceptive services. Those services are as important as ever, though they must adapt to the needs of a new generation of clients. But today's new population challenges require accelerated investment in human development—in particular, investments in girls' education. They also demand fresh attention to the inequities that prevent women—and girls—from freely choosing the number and timing of their children. The next wave of population policies must be far better targeted, emphasize social inclusion, assure the observance of human rights, and, crucially, address the opportunity structures and capacities of young populations—especially young girls. The "unmet need" we must fill now is for justice.

Organizations to Contact

The editors have compiled the following list of organizations concerned with the issues debated in this book. The descriptions are derived from materials provided by the organizations. All have publications or information available for interested readers. The list was compiled on the date of publication of the present volume; names, addresses, phone and fax numbers, and e-mail and Internet addresses may change. Be aware that many organizations take several weeks or longer to respond to inquiries, so allow as much time as possible.

Brookings Institution
1775 Masachusetts Ave. NW, Washington, DC 20036
(202) 797-6000 • fax: (202) 797-6004
website: www.brookings.edu

The Brookings Institution is a think tank that conducts research and education in the areas of foreign policy, economics, government, and the social sciences. Its website features numerous briefings and publications on the topic of the global economy. Examples include *Urban Poverty in Developing Countries: A Scoping Study for Future Research, The Emerging Middle Class in Developing Countries*, and *Continuity and Change: China's Attitude Toward Hard Power and Soft Power.*

Earth Island Institute
2150 Allston Way, Suite 460, Berkeley, CA 94704
(510) 859-9100 • fax: (510) 859-9091
website: www.earthisland.org

Earth Island Institute's work addresses environmental issues and their relation to such concerns as human rights and economic development in the Third World. The institute's publications include the quarterly *Earth Island Journal*. Articles including *The Developing World's 10 Best Ethical Destinations* and *Eco Equity: A Peak on the Horizon*, are available on its website.

Friends of the Earth International
PO Box 19199, 1000 gd, Amsterdam
  The Netherlands
+31 20 622 1369 • fax: +31 20 639 2181
website: www.foei.org

Friends of the Earth International is an international advocacy organization dedicated to protecting the planet from environmental degradation; preserving biological, cultural, and ethnic diversity; and empowering citizens to have an influential voice in decisions affecting the quality of their environment. It has a US chapter and publishes numerous publications dealing with the environment. Recent publications include *Rich Countries Try to Dodge Climate Obligations* and *Climate Change: Rich Nations Backtracking.*

Global Policy Forum (GPF)
777 UN Plaza, Suite 3D, New York, NY   10017
(212) 557-3161 • fax: (212) 557-3165
e-mail: gpf@globalpolicy.org
website: www.globalpolicy.org

Global Policy Forum monitors policy making at the United Nations, promotes accountability of global decisions, educates and mobilizes citizen participation, and advocates on vital issues of international peace and justice. The forum publishes policy papers and the *GPF Newsletter.* On its website GPF provides an internal globalization link with subcategories on the topic, including politics, culture, and economics. The website also provides various news items and articles. Article examples include *Ten Problems with Free Trade, Report Says Developing Nations Lost $6.5 Trillion in Illicit Outflows in Last Decade,* and *Poverty Reduction Is Not Development.*

Global Water
3600 S Harbor Blvd., Suite 514, Oxnard, CA   93035
(805) 985-3057 • fax: (805) 985-3688
e-mail: info@globalwater.org
website: www.globalwater.org

Global Water is an international, nonprofit, nongovernmental organization dedicated to helping provide clean drinking water for developing countries. The organization provides technical assistance, water supply equipment, and volunteers to help poor countries develop safe and effective water supply programs around the world.

Greenpeace

Ottho Heldringstraat 5, 1066 AZ, Amsterdam
  The Netherlands
+31 20 718 2000 • fax: +31 20 514 8151
e-mail: greenpeace.usa@wdc.greenpeace.org
website: www.greenpeace.org

Greenpeace is a global nonprofit organization and advocacy group that focuses on the most crucial worldwide threats to the planet's biodiversity and environment. Its website lists numerous environmental position papers and other publications relating to the developing world and the environment. Recent publications relating to the developing world include *Forests for Climate* and *Industrialized Countries Missing the Target to Avert Runaway Climate Change.*

Institute for Policy Studies (IPS)

1112 Sixteenth St. NW, Suite 600, Washington, DC   20036
(202) 234-9382
e-mail: info@ips-dc.org
website: www.ips-dc.org

The Institute for Policy Studies is a progressive think tank that focuses on national and international peace, justice, and environmental issues. In order to influence policymakers, the press, the public, and key social movements, IPS fellows and associates publish a wide variety of materials, including books, reports, op-eds, commentaries, fact sheets, talking points, speeches, and event transcripts. Recent reports include *Civil Society Responses to the Global Financial and Economic Crisis* and *Mining for Profits in International Tribunals.*

International Monetary Fund (IMF)

700 Nineteenth St. NW, Washington, DC   20431

(202) 623-7000 • fax: (202) 623-4661

e-mail: publicaffairs@imf.org

website: www.imf.org

The IMF is an international organization of 184 member countries. It was established to promote international monetary cooperation, exchange stability, and orderly exchange arrangements. IMF fosters economic growth and high levels of employment and provides temporary financial assistance to countries. It publishes the quarterly *Finance & Development* and reports on its activities, including the quarterly *Global Financial Stability Report*, recent issues of which are available on its website along with data on IMF finances and individual country reports.

International Water Management Institute (IWMI)

PO Box 2075, Colombo
   Sri Lanka

+94 11 288 0000 • fax: +94 11 278 6854

e-mail: iwmi@cgiar.org

website: www.iwmi.cgiar.org

The International Water Management Institute is a nonprofit scientific organization funded by the Consultative Group on International Agricultural Research (CGIAR). IWMI concentrates on water and related land management challenges faced by poor rural communities.

RAND Corporation

1776 Main St., PO Box 2138, Santa Monica, CA   90407-2138

(310) 393-0411 • fax: (310) 393-4818

website: www.rand.org

The RAND Corporation is a nonprofit think tank that conducts research and analysis on national security, business, education health, law, and science. Its website features a "Hot

Topics" section on globalization that provides selected research, commentary, and congressional testimony by RAND experts on the topic.

United Nations Conference on Trade and Development (UNCTAD)

Palais des Nations, 8-14 Av. de la Paix, 1211 Geneva 10
   Switzerland
+41 22 917 1234 • fax: +41 22 917 0057
e-mail: unctadinfo@unctad.org
website: www.unctad.org/

UNCTAD was established by the United Nations (UN) to help integrate developing countries into the world economy. UNCTAD has organized three UN conferences on the least-developed countries, and its Special Programme for Least Developed, Landlocked and Island Developing Countries promotes the socioeconomic development of these countries through research, policy analysis, and technical assistance. Its website contains information about the least-developed countries and links to UN reports and other materials relating to trade issues and development.

United Nations Development Programme (UNDP)

1 United Nations Plaza, New York, NY   10017
(212) 906-5000
website: www.undp.org

UNDP funds six thousand projects in more than 150 developing countries and territories. It works with governments, other United Nations agencies, and nongovernmental organizations to enhance self-reliance and promote sustainable human development. Its priorities include improving living standards, protecting the environment, and applying technology to meet human needs. UNDP's publications include the weekly newsletter *UNDPFlash*, the human development magazine *Choices*, and the annual *UNDPHuman Development Report*. On its wesite, UNDP publishes the *Millennium Development Goals*, its annual report, regional data and analysis, speeches and statements, and recent issues of its publications.

**United Nations Education, Scientific and
Cultural Organization (UNESCO)**

7 place de Fontenoy, Paris 07 SP   75352
    France
+33 (0)1 45 68 10 00 • fax: +33 (0)1 45 67 16 90
website: www.unesco.org

UNESCO is a specialized agency of the United Nations (UN)
that seeks to promote cooperation among member countries
in the areas of education, science, culture, and communication. UNESCO is actively pursuing the UN's Millennium Development Coals, which seek to halve the proportion of people
living in extreme poverty in developing countries by 2015.

World Bank

1818 H St. NW, Washington, DC   20433
(202) 473-1000 • fax: (202) 477-6391
website: www.worldbank.org

Formally known as the International Bank for Reconstruction
and Development (IBRD), the World Bank seeks to reduce
poverty and improve the standards of living of poor people
around the world. It promotes sustainable growth and investments in developing countries through loans, technical assistance, and policy guidance. The website provides current development data and programs.

World Health Organization (WHO)

Avenue Appia 20, Geneva 27   1211
    Switzerland
+41 22 791 2111 • fax: +41 22 791 3111
e-mail: info@who.int
website: www.who.int

The World Health Organization is the United Nations' specialized agency for health. Established in 1948, WHO seeks to
promote the highest possible level of health for all people.
Health is defined in WHO's constitution as a state of com-
plete physical, mental, and social well-being and not merely

the absence of disease or infirmity. WHO is governed by 193 member countries through the World Health Assembly. WHO's website contains a library of WHO reports and publications, as well as links to various world health journals and reports.

World Trade Organization (WTO)

Centre William Rappard, rue de Lausanne 154
Geneva 21 CH-1211
  Switzerland
+41 22 739 5111 • fax: +41 22 731 4206
e-mail: enquiries@wto.org
website: www.wto.org

WTO is a global international organization that establishes rules dealing with the trade between nations. Two WTO agreements have been negotiated and signed by a majority of the world's trading nations and ratified in their parliaments. The goal of these agreements is to help producers of goods and services, exporters, and importers conduct their business. WTO publishes trade statistics, research and analysis, studies, reports, and the journal *World Trade Review*. Recent publications are available on the WTO website.

Worldwatch Institute

1776 Massachusetts Ave. NW, Washington, DC 20036-1904
(202) 452-1999 • fax: (202) 296-7365
e-mail: worldwatch@worldwatch.org
website: www.worldwatch.org

Worldwatch is a research organization that analyzes and calls attention to global problems, including environmental concerns such as the loss of cropland, forests, habitat, species, and water supplies. It compiles the annual *State of the World* anthology and publishes the bimonthly magazine *World Watch* as well as various reports, papers, and other publications. Examples include the report *Renewable Energy and Energy Efficiency in China: Current Status and Prospects for 2020* and a magazine article, *Sustainable Entrepreneurship in Africa.*

Bibliography

Books

Kwame Anthony Appiah	*The Honor Code: How Moral Revolutions Happen.* New York: Norton, 2010.
Ann Bernstein	*The Case for Business in Developing Economies.* New York: Penguin, 2010.
Otaviatio Canuto and Marcelo Giugale	*The Day After Tomorrow: A Handbook on the Future of Economic Policy in the Developing World.* Washington, DC: World Bank, 2010.
Paul Collier	*The Bottom Billion: Why the Poorest Countries Are Failing and What Can Be Done About It.* New York: Oxford University Press, 2008.
Carrie Liu Currier and Manochehr Dorraj	*China's Energy Relations with the Developing World.* New York: Continuum, 2011.
Laura Frost, Michael R. Reich, Tadataka Yamada, and Beth Anne Pratt	*Access: How Do Good Health Technologies Get to Poor People in Poor Countries?* Boston, MA: Harvard Center for Population and Development Studies, 2009.
Laura Frost, Michael R. Reich, Tadataka Yamada, and Beth Anne Pratt	*Politics in the Developing World.* New York: Oxford University Press, 2010.

Ronald Inglehart and Christian Welzel	*How Development Leads to Democracy.* New York: Council on Foreign Affairs, 2009.
Joshua Kurlantzick	*Charm Offensive: How China's Soft Power Is Transforming the World.* New Haven, CT: Yale University Press, 2007.
Mustapha K. Nabli, ed.	*The Great Recession and Developing Countries: Economic Impact and Growth Prospects.* Washington, DC: World Bank, 2011.
Marc Plattner	*Democracy Without Borders? Global Challenges to Liberal Democracy.* Lanham, MD: Rowman & Littlefield, 2008.
Nita Rudra	*Globalization and the Race to the Bottom in Developing Countries: Who Really Gets Hurt?* New York: Cambridge University Press, 2008.
Richard D. Semba and Martin W. Bloem	*Nutrition and Health in Developing Countries.* New York: Humana, 2008.
Gilyn Williams, Paula Meth, and Katie Willis	*Geographies of Developing Areas: The Global South in a Changing World.* New York: Routledge, 2009.
Ronald Wraith and Edgar Simpkins	*Corruption in Developing Countries.* New York: Routledge, 2011.

Vineeta Yadav

Political Parties, Business Groups, and Corruption in Developing Countries. New York: Oxford University Press, 2011.

Periodicals and Internet Sources

Laurel Angrist

"The Top 10 Developing Countries for Sustainable Adventure Tourism," *The Travel Word*, June 10, 2010. www.thetravelword.com.

Barbara Casassus

"Rapidly Developing Countries Are Innovation Champions: Top Emerging Economies Are Forging Research Collaborations to Help the Less Well-Off," *Nature*, December 20, 2010.

Tom Clynes

"Confronting Corruption," *Conservation Magazine*, December 8, 2010.

Guy Collender

"Nations in Conflict Can Benefit from Technology," PublicService.co.uk, March 30, 2010.

Emmanuel K. Dogbevi

"Foreign Direct Investments into Developing Countries to Increase by 17% in 2010—Report," *Ghana Business News*, December 31, 2010. www.ghanabusinessnews.com.

Susan B. Epstein, Nina M. Serafino, and Francis T. Miko

"Democracy Promotion: Cornerstone of U.S. Foreign Policy?" Congressional Research Service, December 26, 2007. http://congressionalresearch.com.

Azar Gat et al.	"Which Way Is History Marching? Debating the Authoritarian Revival," *Foreign Affairs*, July/August 2009.
Ben W. Heineman Jr.	"Where Are the Global Anti-Corruption Leaders?" *Atlantic*, February 10, 2010.
Justmeans	"In 2010, Developing Countries Lead the Way on Wind," CleanTechies, December 13, 2010. http://blog.cleantechies.com.
Martin Khor	"Developing Countries Should Be Paid for Eco Disasters," *Global Geopolitics & Political Economy*, July 29, 2010.
Joel Kotkin	"The New World Order," *Newsweek*, September 26, 2010.
Joshua Kurlantzick	"Democracy in Danger," *Prospect*, May 26, 2010.
Hao Li	"Developing Countries Lose Up to $40 Billion per Year to Corruption," *International Business Times*, December 17, 2010.
Wim Naudé	"Promoting Entrepreneurship in Developing Countries: Policy Challenges," United Nations University, 2010. http://unu.edu.
Deepak Nayyar	"The Financial Crisis, the Great Recession and the Developing World," *Global Policy*, January 2010.

Karen Orenstein   "Developing Countries Resist World
                       Bank Power Play," InDepthNews,
                       2010. www.indepthnews.net.

Michael D. Stroup   "Capitalism, Democracy and
                       Environmental Quality," National
                       Center for Policy Analysis, September
                       2, 2010. www.ncpa.org.

Fareed Zakaria   "How Not to Save the World,"
                       Newsweek, September 20, 2008.

Fareed Zakaria   "Hazardous E-Waste Surging in
                       Developing Countries," *Science Daily*,
                       February 23, 2010.
                       www.sciencedaily.com.

Fareed Zakaria   "World Bank Channels $72bn
                       Assistance to Developing Countries
                       in 2010," *Afrique Avenir*, July 3, 2010.
                       www.afriqueavenir.org.

Index